The Art of
Meditating
on
Scripture

The Art of
Meditating
on
Scripture

Understanding Your Faith, Renewing Your Mind, Knowing Your God

Peter Toon

ZondervanPublishingHouse
Academic and Professional Books
Grand Rapids, Michigan

A Division of HarperCollins*Publishers*

THE ART OF MEDITATING ON SCRIPTURE
Copyright © 1993 by Peter Toon

Requests for information should be addressed to:
Zondervan Publishing House
Academic and Professional Books
Grand Rapids, Michigan 49530

Edited by Leonard G. Goss and Bob Wood
Cover design: Tammy Johnson
Cover photogaph: Andy Caulfield, The Image Bank

Library of Congress Cataloging-in-Publication Data
Toon, Peter, 1939–
      The art of meditating on Scripture: understanding your faith, renewing your mind, knowing your God / Peter Toon.
          p.   cm.
      Includes index.
      ISBN 0-310-57761-6
      1. Bible–Devotional Use.   2. Meditation–Christianity
      3. Contemplation.   4. Mysticism.   I. Title.
      BS617.8.T66   1993
      248.3'4–dc20   92-40953
                                                                                CIP

Printed in the United States of America

93 94 95 96 97 98 / ML / 10 9 8 7 6 5 4 3 2 1

For
John and Diane Ott

of the
Prayer Book Society

CONTENTS

PREFACE

I arrived in the United States from England on January 1, 1991, to teach theology at the Episcopal (Anglican) seminary in Wisconsin called Nashotah House, which this year of 1992 is celebrating its one hundred fiftieth year of operation. Although I have written many short articles since then, this is my first book written wholly within America. Its general theme, however, has been constantly before me for several years.

What I think I see happening in the mainline denominations both in Europe and America is a new alignment. While official ecumenism proceeds through much talking between representatives of denominations, a more dynamic ecumenism is occurring in all the churches. A new line is being drawn through both the Roman Catholic and Protestant churches that sets the modern liberals with their secularist religion on the one side and the modern orthodox with their commitment to revealed, scriptural religion on the other side. Of course there are varieties and shades of secularist religion as there are of scriptural religion, but within the variety are two recognizable religions. Then, of course, one finds church members who are caught in the middle with one foot in each, as it were. Therefore, many people confess today that they have more in common with members of other denominations than their own. And this is true for both the secularists and the scripturalists.

This phenomenon of two religions, with some people hanging on to both as far as they are able, is a reality (a painful one, I find) in the Episcopal Church in the United States. It may also be seen and felt in the Roman Catholic, United Methodist, and Evangelical Lutheran churches, to name only three. Not only does it mean that an orthodox believer has more in common with fellow believers in other denominations, but also that the historic division of high church and low church and even Catholic and Protestant has become of much less importance. The confession of Jesus as Lord and the submission to the authority of the Scriptures and to the teaching of the Nicene Creed unite believers across or through what once seemed to be major or invincible barriers.

In a sense this book reflects this new ecumenism. I present evidence to show that the saints from the major Christian traditions are truly one as they pray and particularly as they pray contemplatively, looking to the exalted Lord Jesus and through him to the Father.

Various people at Nashotah House have helped me with the work of writing. I wish to thank Sherri Baker, Crews Giles, and Patrick Smith for their technical help, and Professor Charles Caldwell and my wife, Vita, for discussing with me some of the themes presented in the book.

In my own mind I associate this book with a book on liturgy I wrote recently, *Knowing God Through the Liturgy* (Prayer Book Society of the Episcopal Church, U.S.A., 1992). And I dedicate this book to the Director of the Prayer Book Society, John Ott, and to his wife, Diane. May our Lord bless them abundantly in their important work.

Peter Toon
Nashotah House
Advent 1992

CHAPTER 1

Evangelical and Catholic

The purpose of this book is practical. It is to encourage Christians to know God the Father experientially as their covenant God, to contemplate Jesus Christ in his heavenly glory by faith and with delight and love, and to walk in the Holy Spirit to fulfill the desires of the Spirit. This is another way of saying that I write to encourage my readers to love the Lord their God with all their heart, mind, soul, and strength, and out of this love to love their neighbors as well.

It is a book about the relationship of faith and prayer— not prayer in general but mental, affective, mystical, and contemplative prayer. One of its themes is that when a person truly believes in the Lord Jesus Christ, that person is called by God to maturity in faith, which includes the practice of meditation and contemplation. This call to be holy, to be perfect, to be sanctified, and to be mature in faith, hope, and love is a call that the Gospel addresses to all who confess Jesus as Lord. Thus, it is addressed both to male and female as well as to clergy and laity. There are no exceptions, for God calls all to holiness and perfection. In responding to this call God treats each one of us differently, for he deals with us as persons with personalities. And none of us is identical with any other.

MEDITATING AND CONTEMPLATING

This is my first book chiefly devoted to contemplating the Lord God and having mystical experience of him as a Christian duty. I say *Christian* duty because it is biblical. I have published several books on the divine art of meditating upon the Bible (e.g., *From Mind to Heart* (1987) and *Meditating As a Christian* (1991). My purpose in writing these was to help Christians discover the biblical and Western Christian habit and methods of meditation upon Holy Scripture. Also, I had an educational task—to contrast biblical meditation with that very different form of so-called meditation that comes from Hinduism and Buddhism, which is found in the New Age movement and which has been adopted, often unwittingly, by orthodox Christians who did not know that there is a distinctly Christian way of meditation.

In writing this book I have taken for granted most of what I have previously written. The reason is that my purpose here is to deal with what may be called the fruit of genuine biblical meditation—fellowship, communion, and union with God the Father through God the Son and by God the Holy Spirit. The knowing of God in prayer has been and is still called both contemplation and mysticism, especially in the Greek Orthodox and Western Catholic (medieval and modern Roman) traditions of spirituality. In contrast Protestants have been hesitant to speak of mysticism, but have been generally happy to speak of contemplation, fellowship, communion, experience, and knowledge of God. (Why Protestants have this hesitancy will be explained in chapter six.)

If I were asked to give one example of mystical experience and prayer that would be meaningful to Christians of varying types, I would choose that of the great Frenchman Blaise Pascal. After his death friends found stitched into the lining of his doublet a scrap of parchment with a rough drawing of a flaming cross. Around that cross were the following words, which recalled an unforgettable experience of the living God:

> In the year of grace 1654 Monday, 23 November, the day of St Clement, Pope and Martyr . . . from about half-past ten in the evening till about half an hour after midnight.

FIRE

> God of Abraham, God of Isaac, God of Jacob,
>   Not of the philosophers and the learned.
> Certitude. Joy. Certitude. Emotion. Sight. Joy.
>   Forgetfulness of the world and of all outside of God.
> The world hath not known Thee, but I have known Thee.
>   Joy! joy! joy! Tears of joy.
> My God, wilt Thou leave me?
>   Let me not be separated from Thee for ever.

> (A facsimile is in Abbé Bremond's *Sentiment Religieux en France*, iv.368.)

Here the master of language is lost for words, but his incoherence points to his encounter with the living God.

If I could add a second example from within mainline Protestantism, I would choose the testimony of Jonathan Edwards (1703–1758), the great philosopher-theologian and author of the spiritual classic, *A Treatise Concerning Religious Affections* (1746). In his *Personal Narrative*, published after his death, he wrote:

> Once, as I rode out into the woods for my health, in 1737, having alighted from my horse in a retired place, as my manner commonly had been to walk for divine contemplation and prayer, I had a view that for me was extraordinary, of the glory of the Son of God, as Mediator between God and man, and his wonderful, great, full, pure and sweet grace and love, and meek and gentle condescension. This grace that appeared so calm and sweet, appeared also great above the heavens. The person of Christ appeared ineffably excellent with an

excellency great enough to swallow up all thought and conception . . . which continued near as I can judge, about an hour; which kept me the greater part of the time in a flood of tears and weeping aloud. I felt an ardency of soul to be, what I know not otherwise how to express, emptied and annihilated; to lie in the dust, and to be full of Christ alone; to love him with a holy and pure love; to trust in him; to live upon him; to serve and follow him; and to be perfectly sanctified and made pure, with a divine and heavenly purity. I have, several other times, had views very much of the same nature, and which have had the same effects.

This could be called affective prayer, the contemplation of the heart. Edwards continues:

I have many times had a sense of the glory of the third Person in the Trinity, in his office as Sanctifier; in his holy operations, communicating divine light and life to the soul. God, in the communications of his Holy Spirit, has appeared as an infinite fountain of divine glory and sweetness; being full, and sufficient to fill and satisfy the soul; pouring forth itself in sweet communications; like the sun in its glory, sweetly and pleasantly diffusing light and life. And I have sometimes had an affecting sense of the excellency of the Word of God, as a word of life; as the light of life; a sweet, excellent, lifegiving word; accompanied with a thirsting after that word, that it might dwell richly in my heart. (*Personal Narrative* in *Works*, 1808 ed. vol. 1.)

Edwards, like Pascal, was a master of words. But he, too, was fully stretched to give an account of his experience of the living God.

My treatment of the theme of contemplation is intended to be primarily biblical. In fact I pay particular attention to the letter to the Romans in order to show that in the very document where the apostle Paul sets forth the liberating doctrine of justification by faith, he includes a call to sanctification, holiness, maturity in faith, and spiritual or heavenly mindedness. An essential part of the road to this maturity in faith is contemplative prayer. Paul certainly believed and taught that those whom God justifies by faith ought to be those who are wholly dedicated to the service of the Lord Jesus Christ in the obedience of faith. In fact those who truly live by faith are also those who know God experientially in faith and faithfulness as they seek his face and as they are guided by the Spirit of Christ in prayer and in the practical obedience of faith.

While I seek to submit to Holy Scripture as the sole authority for faith and conduct, I also pray and minister within a specific tradition of Western Christianity. I am an Anglican Christian and an ordained presbyter/priest of the Church of England. This means, as the title of one of my books indicates (*The Anglican Way: Evangelical and Catholic*, 1983), that I see myself as a member of a church where we are called both to submit to Holy Scripture and also to receive from tradition guidance for doctrine (via creeds), worship (via liturgies), and spirituality (via collections of prayers and devotions). So it will not surprise my reader to find me speaking approvingly of forms of prayer that technically belong to what may be called the Eastern Orthodox and Western Catholic traditions of spirituality. Within my cultural skins, which I cannot shed, as an Englishman and Britisher, I seek to be both biblical and traditional, dynamic and conservative in my exposition of the place of contemplation in the obedience of faith in the God and Father of our Lord Jesus Christ. However, I have tried my very best to understand American culture and the American mindset and to write in such a way as to communicate with fellow Christians whose cultural skins are different from my own. I hope I have succeeded.

I assume that there are four elements in Christianity, all of which are to be held together. There is the fact of belonging to the fellowship of faith, the church with its order and worship; there is the exercise, according to ability, of the intellectual element of doctrine and theological reflection; there is the practical element of serving God in his world, which includes evangelism and loving the neighbor; finally, there is the personal, experiential element of knowing God as Father and Jesus as Lord. If the last element is cultivated alone, in an individualistic way, then a strong possibility exists that spiritual life will be warped and imbalanced. True contemplation is of course a highly personal activity, but it ought to be the prayer of the person who is an integral part of the household of faith and of the body of Christ and who with fellow Christians is pressing onward in grace to the maturity of faith, hope, and love.

SAINTS EVERYWHERE!

We normally call by the name of saints those Christians who have obeyed the Lord Jesus, embodied the love of God in their lives, and allowed the Spirit to fill and guide them. In fact, following the example of the apostle Paul we can claim that every Christian is a saint, in the sense that in Jesus Christ he or she is set apart from sin to the service of God and thus has begun the way of holiness. Yet few Christians seem to become in real practical terms what they are already, in potential and by the grace of God, in Christ. And these few to whom we give the title *saint* come from all the major traditions of the one, holy, catholic, and apostolic church of God. Of course Roman Catholics have an elaborate procedure for determining whether or not a person truly is to be called a saint, but in ordinary Christian discourse we use the word *saint* of those whom we believe truly to have walked with the Lord Jesus, reflecting his character and virtues.

I have often asked myself why it is that saints appear and thrive in their glorifying of God in all the branches of Christendom. How can it be that saints are continually being produced within contexts that are judged by some Christians to be theologically heretical or in serious error? For example, Protestants have accused the Roman Catholic Church of teaching false doctrine, and Roman Catholics have accused

Protestants of being heretics. But saints have appeared and continue to appear in both of these branches of Christendom.

Part of the explanation for this lies in the relation of experience and doctrine. Saints are those who truly experience God in his mercy and grace and respond to his gracious mercy in faith, hope, and love. They are people who know God experientially as the living God with whom they are in vital communion. Doctrine is not the primary reality in their lives but is that form of words by which they communicate, express, and preserve their vital experience of God. Certainly what they are taught in their respective churches and/or denominations has an effect on them, but saints take most seriously the call (which is clearly set forth in all major branches of Christendom) to believe and trust in God through Jesus Christ, to love him with heart, soul, mind, and strength, and to love their neighbors as they love themselves.

So while their external ways of worship are different and while they express their experience of God in differing doctrinal statements, they are united in their wholehearted dedication and commitment to the One God in Trinity, to the Incarnation of the eternal Son and his sacrifice of Atonement at Calvary, to the presence and power of the Holy Spirit in the church, and to pressing on toward maturity in faith, hope, and love. Saints do not merely know about God through doctrinal systems, but they know God intimately as their Lord with whom they are united in fellowship in his covenant of grace. In fact some saints know little doctrine, but know God personally in a profound way. Their knowledge of God is not primarily knowledge about him but the knowledge of acquaintance with him. They know him because they are often with him and he with them.

Doctrines are constructions put together by Christians in order to bring into harmony and order the multidimensioned expression of divine revelation in Holy Scripture. Obviously some constructions are better than others and some are false whereas others are true. Virtually all Christians subscribe to the doctrines of God as One God in Trinity and to Jesus as the Incarnate Son of God, just as these are presented in the ancient creeds. Saints are those who are in mystical communion with this God, for they come to the Father through the Son by the Holy Spirit to adore, praise, trust, obey, and serve him. We are all called to be saints, and, as I shall argue, there is no way to genuine saintliness that does not include genuine contemplative, mystical prayer. The mind must, as it were, descend into the heart and then the whole soul ascend to seek for and gaze upon the majesty of God.

THE STRUCTURE

The study begins with an analysis and reflection upon Romans 12:1–2. At this point in his long letter, the apostle recalls what he has taught in chapters 1–11 concerning God's mercy; on that basis he calls for total dedication to the will of God in daily living. Such consecration means that Christians are not conformed to this present age and its values, but are being transformed by the renewing of the basic structure of their thinking. We note that such renewing requires not only meditation on God's mercy but also contemplation of and mystical union with the God of mercy himself as he is known in Jesus Christ. Thus one of the major themes of the book, contemplation, is raised through reflecting upon the call to holiness.

In the next chapter the emphasis is upon the major manifestation of God's mercy, his righteousness, which is revealed in the gospel, centers on Jesus Christ, and is received by faith. We pay close attention to several important passages. First of all Romans 1:16–17, where Paul provides a summary of the major themes of the letter—in particular, righteousness and faith. Then we also turn to Romans 3:21–26, where Paul explains the relationship of God's righteousness, human faith, and Christ's sacrificial death at Calvary. Through this biblical exegesis we gain an insight into the Pauline doctrine of justification by faith, and begin to understand that it is teaching about the living God who places believing sinners in his covenant of grace, and then having placed them there keeps them within this relationship of mercy by his covenant faithfulness. Therefore, in chapter three, two more major themes of his book are brought into view—faith and our being reckoned righteous before (i.e., in covenant with) God.

We stay within the letter to Rome in chapter four. Here we explore Paul's account of the growth in faith to maturity in faithfulness and love through walking in the Spirit and being spiritually minded. Here we are drawn particularly to Romans 8, where Paul reflects upon the nature of true Christian living and experience of God. Again we examine and develop the themes of faith and meditation/contemplation in the knowing and loving of God, since spiritual mindedness (for which Paul calls) includes contemplation.

In chapter five we begin to reflect seriously upon the nature and practice of meditation. This reflection begins by studying Paul's own meditative approach and moves out from there to look at meditation in the Bible and Christian practice. Doing this we come to see that what Protestants have included in meditation is often rather more than Roman Catholics have. In fact some, if not all, of what is known as contemplation in the Catholic tradition is covered in the Protestant tradition under different headings (e.g., communion with God, knowing God, experience of God, heavenly mindedness, and so on). Not a few Protestant teachers of meditation treat meditation and contemplation as synonyms, and so include in meditation much of what the Catholic tradition places in contemplation.

Having examined the practice of meditation, we turn in chapter six to seek to identify what is meant by contemplation. This is done by examination of biblical teaching as well as by reflection upon the development of mysticism/contemplation in the history of the church. Since a distinguished company of German and Scandinavian theologians has claimed that the mystical tradition is a move away from biblical, prophetic prayer, some space is given to reflecting upon and answering this charge, which represents, I think, a prejudiced reading of the evidence.

All agree that the one theologian of the early church who most influenced both Roman Catholicism and Protestantism was St. Augustine of Hippo. He has been called "the prince of mystics." Therefore, in chapter seven we look briefly at his teaching on contemplation, which has a strong intellectual element to it while also being a passionate expression of longing for God. As a contrast we also notice the "contemplation of the heart" of St. Bernard of Clairvaux.

Chapter eight is given over to the exposition of meditation/contemplation in the writings of John Owen (1616–1683), the English Puritan theologian who was the dean of Christ Church, Oxford, from 1651 to 1660. In 1973 the publisher of this book made available my biography of Owen under the title *God's Statesman*. Owen was not only a deep thinker, but also a man who took very seriously the call to be holy. His writings on the life of faith are not popular books, but they are filled with profound insight into the meaning of Scripture. He certainly knew what it is to know God in contemplative prayer, and his views may be said to represent a high point in Protestant development and exposition of what was often called "the divine art of meditation and contemplation." In this chapter also we notice briefly the teaching of Richard Baxter, a famous contemporary of Owen, in order to show that there was a common Protestant approach to contemplation that centered upon looking by faith upon the exalted Lord Jesus in heaven.

The stage is set to look in chapter nine at the teaching of a well known and highly influential exponent of contemplation, St. Teresa of Avila, the sixteenth-century Carmelite nun.

Though her exposition does not have the theological weight or learning of John Owen, it is based upon careful analysis of her own life of prayer and that of others, and it is set within the late-medieval tradition of teaching on prayer and the theological virtues, available at that time in the convents of Spain. Her influence as a teacher of contemplation has been immense within the Catholic world.

Chapter ten is devoted to the Orthodox Way, the path of contemplation developed in the Orthodox churches of the eastern Mediterranean and Russia. This has its own particular context and emphasis, which is proving attractive to a great number of Western Christians today. In particular we examine the use of the Jesus Prayer and notice the relation of contemplation to the Eucharist.

Finally, in chapter eleven I attempt to pull together the major insights and teaching concerning the relation of faith and contemplation. This is done to encourage the reader to believe that the Lord is calling him/her to the practice of contemplation as part of God's work of renewing the mind and bringing holiness, consecration, and sanctification to the church and each member of it.

In an appendix I supply an annotated book list for those who wish to follow up any theme from the eleven chapters.

THE COVENANT OF GRACE

Already I have used the word *covenant* to explain the contents of the book. It is such an important concept in the Bible that we cannot escape from it when we are thinking of our relationship to God through Jesus Christ our Lord. The relationship of God with Abraham, the people of Israel, the new Israel (the church), and with all who receive Jesus as the Lord and Christ is that of a covenant relationship. However, this is no ordinary covenant; it is not an agreement between two equal or near-equal sets of partners. It is a covenant of grace.

God begins the relationship as he declares, "I will establish my covenant" (Gen. 6:18; Ex. 6:4–5). Then the essence of the covenant is captured by his effectual word: "I will be your God and you will be my people" (Gen. 17:7; Rev. 21:2–3). Thus while the covenant is unilateral in its origin and establishment, it is two-sided when it comes into being. The recipients of the covenant become by God's choice and mercy covenant partners of God; their duty is to love, worship, and serve the Lord their God and to keep his commandments (Deut. 7:9, 12; 1 Kings 8:23).

God established this covenant of grace with Abraham (Gen. 17:7) and his descendants; then at Sinai and through Moses the Lord God established a particular form of this same covenant with the people of Israel. Much of the Five Books of Moses—Genesis through Deuteronomy—presents the content of the covenant in terms of both the covenantal duties of the Israelites and the promises of faithfulness from God himself. In the rest of the Old Testament we read of God's continuing faithfulness to his covenant people and the Israelites' constant failure to be the kind of covenant partners God looked for. They failed not only because of their creatureliness and finitude but also because of their sinfulness and pride.

In and through Jesus Christ God established a new covenant—that is, a new expression of the one covenant of grace. This had been promised by the prophets in the old or Mosaic covenant. When it was inaugurated through the sacrificial death and atonement of Jesus, it displaced the old administration of the covenant. In every way this new covenant is a more wonderful manifestation of God's covenant mercy and faithfulness, as the Letter to the Hebrews makes abundantly clear. It is based on the saving, reconciling work of God in the Lord Jesus. Those who are brought into it and maintained in its embrace are given the gift of the indwelling Spirit, who guides them into the way of obedience and of the fulfilling of their covenantal duties, both as God's partners and as his children.

Paul makes it clear that two of the great benefits of membership of the new covenant are justification (being declared to be, and placed in, a right relationship with God) and sanctification (the gift of the indwelling Spirit, both to assure membership of the new covenant and to help fulfill the duties of a covenant partner). Of these I shall have much to say in later chapters. And, as we shall see, a part of the renewing of the mind to which Paul calls all believers is the understanding and internal digesting of the truth from God in his Gospel, which is expressed in the concepts of justification and sanctification.

Meanwhile, it is perhaps necessary to emphasize that though God himself in grace both established and maintains the covenant of grace with his believing and faithful people, he does actually adopt them as his children (as Romans 8 declares). That is, he does not merely treat them as inferior and weak covenant partners upon whom he has had mercy, but he delights in them as his children and desires to have fellowship and communion with them. This is the sphere in which we shall place and discuss the role of contemplation: it is prayerful, mystical communing with their heavenly Father through his Son, the Lord Jesus, in which believing and faithful adopted children engage.

CHAPTER 2

Renewing the Mind

*I*n recent decades we have heard much about renewal in our churches. This usually points to the charismatic movement and the recovery of the supernatural gifts of the Spirit within the worship, fellowship, and evangelism of congregations.

LIFE IN THE SPIRIT

There is another dimension to renewal of the church, the renewal of the mindset, or the basic theological thinking patterns of Christians in a secular world. It is of such renewal that Paul speaks in Romans 12:1–2:

> Therefore, I urge you, brothers, in view of God's mercy, to offer your bodies as living sacrifices, holy and pleasing to God—this is your spiritual act of worship. Do not conform any longer to the pattern of this world, but be transformed by the renewing of your mind. Then you will be able to test and approve what God's will is— his good, pleasing and perfect will.

This renewal, like all renewal for the apostle, is the work of God and specifically the work of the Holy Spirit. He acts in the name and with the virtues of Jesus Christ, and so Paul calls him "the Spirit of Christ" (8:9). The proof that renewal is occurring will be the full recognition of the will of God with a desire and commitment to do it day by day. For it is only a renewed mind that can recognize the perfect will of God.

Before ascertaining what the renewal of the mind involves, it will be convenient first of all to note the context of renewal. The full background is "God's mercy," which has been described in Romans 1–11. Renewal is to occur because God has both revealed himself through, and reconciled quilty sinners to himself in Jesus Christ. God's mercy is particularly evident in the sacrificial death of Jesus on the cross, in his glorious resurrection from the dead, in his exaltation into heaven (8:31–39), and in the presence and power of the Holy Spirit in the hearts of the society of believers.

In response to God's mercy believers are urged by Paul to offer themselves to him as living, bodily sacrifices. Such a daily, complete offering is both a spiritual act (prompted by the Holy Spirit) and a rational act (such mercy calls for and is rightly served by total dedication). It is the movement of a person's inward being toward God, which results in his or her total bodily commitment. And it is also an act of worship that is offered to the God who is supremely worthy to receive our total homage, praise, and adoration (cf. Rom. 6:12ff.).

Having urged obedience in response to the mercies of God, Paul proceeds to make a further exhortation based upon what may be called an eschatological framework: In Jesus, the Christ, the new epoch or age has dawned, and though this new age will not replace the present age until the Second Coming of Christ to judge the nations, it is made present and effective within the present age by the work of the Spirit of God in the church and world. It is invisible now but known through "the firstfruits of the Spirit" (Rom. 8:23) in the dynamic experience of the living God in the Christian congregation.

Therefore, being aware of the realm of the Holy Spirit, Paul urges believers not to adopt either popular or sophisticated patterns of Graeco-Roman culture as the basis for their lifestyle and morals. To be conformed to this age/world results in an "unfit mind" (1:28). Paul certainly recognized the power of social groups, cultural norms, institutions and traditions to mold patterns of behavior. To participate in Christ's act of redemption means the renewing of the mind by the Spirit of Christ. Elsewhere (Titus 3:5) Paul taught that renewal is begun in baptism (see also 2 Cor. 4:16 and Col. 3:10). Here Paul calls for the renewal of human nature because the old age of sin and death is on its way out and the new age of righteousness and joy in the Holy Spirit is at hand. Thus, the renewal begun in baptism/conversion is actually advanced with every genuinely Christian decision/act and moved to its fulfillment in the glory of God in the glorious age to come with the Second Coming of the Lord Jesus Christ to judge the world.

MIND

When Paul speaks of "mind" here, he uses a singular noun–*nous*. That is, he speaks of the renewal of the one mind of the one congregation of believers in Rome. *Nous* can mean "reason" or the rational faculty of human beings, but this is hardly the primary meaning here. Rather, the apostle speaks of what is popularly called the "mind-set." He refers to the basic foundation, structure, and content of the church's thinking. This body of baptized believers is to have a common mind in that they are to think *theologically;* in other words they are so to think and reason (*logos*) that God (*theos*), the God of mercy and the God and Father of our Lord Jesus Christ, is truly the center of their hearts and lives.

In our culture, concern for the esteem and preservation

of self and for those near and dear tends to dominate everyday thinking. Such thinking need not mean the elimination of thinking about God, just as it does not require that there be no thought of the needs of the poor and the destitute. The concern over *nous* goes to the very basis and the actual structure of thinking. Paul does not call merely for religious thinking but for thinking that begins, progresses, and ends in the glory of God. It is to have the mind of Christ, whose own thinking, as reflected in his life, was to glorify God and do the will of the Father who sent him.

Thus, Paul's exhortation applies to the whole body of believers; they are to think theologically after the example and with the mind of Christ as they worship, have fellowship, and serve the Lord together. Their thinking is to be both structured and informed by revealed truth from God so that the way they relate to each other and work together stands in marked contrast to the way most people think and act in human society. Their common life and testimony is certainly not to conform to the pattern of the pagan world around them but to the will of God revealed through his mercy, recorded in sacred Scripture, and conveyed by the apostolic teaching.

Perhaps I need to make clear that Paul is not envisaging a democracy where each member first studies a topic and then all return to take a vote in order to determine what is the mind of Christ. Rather, he is thinking of a congregation led and guided by elders (or presbyters or bishops) to whom the congregation is submitted in love and humility. Therefore, a great responsibility in producing genuine theological thinking in the congregation rests upon the elders through teaching and example.

Further, each Christian (female and male, slave and free), though certainly a member of the one body of Christ, is also as a person individually responsible to God the Father through Jesus the Lord. Each has, and all together have a solemn duty to be renewed in mind through the mercy of

God and by the action of the Holy Spirit. For that to which God calls the whole body he calls each of the members, yet his call is first to the body and through and in the body to each individual. The renewed mind is never individualistic; it does not think in terms only of God and self but of God, the body of Christ, and self as a member of the body.

Today Western Christians have to be particularly watchful in their thinking about God and themselves because of the power of modern secularist culture to warp Christian thinking and teaching. Careless and sloppy thinking can be a major hindrance to renewal and holiness. Take, for example, the common claims made on behalf of feelings, especially in American society: "This is how I feel" and "get in touch with your feelings," with the presumption that feelings are the most important aspect of human experience. Too many of us tend to think from within our feelings, which is another way of saying that our thinking is not so careful and exact as it ought to be because it is determined by powerful emotions. Thus, we either miss the truth or do not rightly understand the truth when it is presented to us; so we cannot genuinely apply the truth to our lives. We apply half-truths! Of course there is a full place for the emotions, feelings, affections, but they are not to replace the rational mind.

Another, not unrelated, matter is the way we tend to think about ourselves as human beings. What I am pointing to is captured in two words, "person" and "individual," and their different meanings. We define an individual in terms of separation from other individuals; we define a person in terms of relations with other persons. The church is a fellowship of persons, who are united in communion one with another and with their Lord. As such they can have one *nous*, because in and by the Holy Spirit they have "the mind of Christ." However, if we think of the church as a society of individuals, then we are promoting the rights of individual opinion and unchecked private judgment rather than the cultivation of a common unity in the Lord Jesus.

To be governed primarily by feelings, or to be under the misunderstanding that individualism is Christian, are ways in which contemporary culture distorts Christian insight and fellowship. It is not easy to stand against the tide. Obviously, what Paul called for in the Roman church cannot be described as easy to accomplish, for it was a call to swim against the tide of Graeco-Roman culture, which produced or encouraged a very different mind-set from that of the Gospel. In fact there would have been in Rome, as in any large city then, a variety of mind-sets. There were varieties in paganism then as there are in secularism today. Underlying the variety, Paul taught, is the fact of a fallen human race and the existence in each of us of a sinful mind-set.

Earlier in this letter Paul had given his reflections upon the state of the pagan world of the Roman Empire: "Since they did not think it worthwhile to retain the knowledge of God, he [God] gave them over to a depraved mind, to do what ought not to be done" (1:28). His point was that there is a revelation of and from God in the natural world and in human conscience but that human beings have not acted upon this revelation. They have rejected it, preferring to follow the inclinations of their evil hearts into both idolatry and immorality.

In chapter 8 the apostle contrasted two ways of life, one arising from sinful human nature and the other flowing out of renewed or regenerate human nature. He wrote:

> Those who live according to the sinful nature have their minds set on what that nature desires; but those who live in accordance with the Spirit have their minds set on what the Spirit desires. The mind of sinful man is death, but the mind controlled by the Spirit is life and peace; the sinful mind is hostile to God. It does not submit to God's law, nor can it do so. Those controlled by the sinful nature cannot please God (vv. 5–8).

Other translations render *sarx* as "flesh," not "sinful nature." A life that is determined by the flesh is more than living a bodily, physical existence on earth; it is also the fixing of attention and desires upon all that satisfies the flesh. Thus, it is to have one's gaze focused upon this world and this world only. In contrast, a life determined by the Spirit of God is to be attentive to and desirous of the invisible realm—the kingdom of God, the exalted Lord Jesus Christ in glory. It is to have one's gaze upon God the Father through God the Son in and by the Holy Spirit. We shall return to this theme later on.

In Romans 8 the noun *nous* is not used. Instead, Paul uses the verb *phroneo* (to set one's mind upon) and the noun *phronēma* (mentality, way of thinking). Thus, Paul is not speaking of the mind-set of the congregation but rather that upon which we set our minds. If we belong entirely to this evil age and world, our minds focus only on this age. However, if we belong through spiritual regeneration to the age to come, the new creation, our minds focus on the One who is the center of this new age and creation, the exalted Lord Jesus Christ.

The reason for the renewal of the mind is clear. Being sinful and hostile to God's gracious will, the mind needs (thus we need) reorientation by the Holy Spirit. This truth is underlined in the letter to Ephesus where Paul refers to pagans being "darkened in their understanding and separated from the life of God because of the ignorance that is in them due to the hardening of their hearts" (4:18; see also v. 17). And the same truth is reiterated in the Pastoral Letters where the human mind is said to be corrupt, depraved, and impure (1 Tim. 6:5; 2 Tim. 3:8; Titus 1:15).

WISDOM FROM THE HOLY SPIRIT

The place of the Holy Spirit in the renewal of the mind and transformation of the soul is crucial. Perhaps in no place does Paul so clearly state it as in 1 Corinthians 2:6–16. Before this particular section of the letter the apostle has made crystal clear that the wisdom of God, in contrast to the wisdom of the Jews or Greeks, is the wisdom revealed in the suffering and death of the Lord of glory upon the cross. "We preach Christ crucified: a stumbling block to Jews and foolishness to Gentiles, but to those whom God has called, both Jews and Greeks, Christ the power of God and the wisdom of God" (1:22). The wisdom of God declared in the Gospel is thus completely and totally different from any human wisdom from anywhere at all!

Thus Paul wrote that "we speak of God's secret wisdom, a wisdom that has been hidden and that God destined for our glory before time began" (2:6); however, none of the rulers, Jewish or Roman, perceived this wisdom revealed in Jesus of Nazareth, so they rejected him. In fact no one, by the use of the mind alone, can see this divine wisdom in the crucified Messiah. Paul humbly admitted that "God has revealed it to us by his Spirit" (2:10). He continued:

> The Spirit searches all things, even the deep things of God. For who among men knows the thoughts of a man except the man's spirit within him? In the same way no one knows the thoughts of God except the Spirit of God. We have not received the spirit of the world but the Spirit who is from God, that we may understand what God has freely given us. This is what we speak, not in words taught us by human wisdom but in words taught by the Spirit, expressing spiritual truths in spiritual words. The man without the Spirit does not accept the things that come from the Spirit of God, for they are foolishness to him, and he cannot understand them, because they are spiritually discerned. The spiritual man makes judgments about all things, but he himself is not subject to any man's judgment:
>
> "For who has known the mind of the Lord
>   that he may instruct him?"
>
> But we have the mind of Christ.

We must consider three important points as we reflect upon these words.

First of all what God did for us and what God revealed of himself to us in the passion and crucifixion of the Lord Jesus is the essence of Christianity. What God revealed and did in the Cross he revealed and did nowhere else. What can be learned of God through the Cross cannot be learned anywhere else. And what can be received via and from the Cross can be received nowhere else. The divine wisdom of Calvary is unique and thus stands in contrast to and in opposition to all other claims to wisdom.

In the second place, the communication of this divine wisdom, and the salvation that comes in and with it, depend upon the agency of the Holy Spirit. Human words and descriptions are insufficient unless they are being used by the Holy Spirit, who knows the mind of God and can communicate the content of that infinite mind to our finite minds and souls.

Finally, the gift of the Holy Spirit to all believing Christians within the body of Christ leads to a special status of Christians vis-à-vis the world (not within the church itself). The presence of the Spirit should identify the local church in such a way that its values and worldview are radically different from the wisdom of the age. The members of the household of faith do know what God has done and is doing in the Lord Jesus Christ; they are living out the life of the future (the age to come) within the present age, which is passing away, and they are marked with the Cross forever. As such, it is clear that they are the temple or the people of the Holy Spirit, who by grace stand in bold contrast to those who live "after the flesh" (Rom. 8:5, KJV)—those who are merely human because they do not appreciate the scandal of the Cross. To be spiritual is not to be elitist; it is to have a deep appreciation of God's profound mystery—salvation through a crucified Messiah (we return to the important theme of "mystery" in chapter six).

PRAYER

Renewal of the mind by the Holy Spirit in theological thinking as described above is not the same as that which is usually understood as theology in our universities. To think theologically today usually means to think rationally and to be able to understand, analyze, and discuss the major doctrines that professional theologians have set out and expounded over the centuries. Such thinking is often merely cerebral or intellectual, being only academic in nature and belonging specifically to the rational faculty.

In contrast, the theological mind formed through the effects of the mercy of God, which is the mind being renewed, involves much more than bare reason. It is the renewing of the mind that is in the heart and is thus the renewal of the very center of human personality. The truth that is being absorbed by the mind is the truth that comes from God within a covenantal and thus personal relationship with him. It is not merely ideas about God but a communion with God in which concepts of God arising from the wisdom revealed in the Cross are dynamic and sanctifying. It is thinking about God in the presence of God and for the glory of God and all done in the name of and within the lordship of Jesus over his church.

The apostle Paul not only called for the renewing of the mind; he also prayed that this would occur in the congregations to which he wrote. For example, this was his prayer and that of his assistant, Timothy, for the church in Colossae (1:9–11).

> . . . we have not stopped praying for you and asking God to fill you with the knowledge of his will through all spiritual wisdom and understanding. And we pray this in order that you may live a life worthy of the Lord and may please him in every way: bearing fruit in every good work, growing in the knowledge of God, being strengthened with all power. . . .

To be filled with spiritual wisdom and understanding is to be renewed in mind. And to this theme Paul returned in the second chapter where he again prayed that "they may have the full riches of complete understanding, in order that they may know the mystery of God, namely, Christ, in whom are hidden all the treasures of wisdom and knowledge" (vv. 2–3).

The theme is perhaps more explicit in Paul's record of his prayer in Ephesians 1:17–19.

> I keep asking that the God of our Lord Jesus Christ, the glorious Father, may give you the Spirit of wisdom and revelation, so that you may know him better. I pray also that the eyes of your heart may be enlightened in order that you may know the hope to which he has called you, the riches of his glorious inheritance in the saints, and his incomparably great power for us who believe.

The apostle desires that they genuinely mature in the knowledge and love of God through the mercy of God the Father, the saving work of Jesus Christ, and the presence in the soul (mind/heart) of the Holy Spirit.

So we may summarize by saying that the renewal of the mind according to God's own wisdom is a basic and fundamental requirement of genuine Christian existence, spirituality, worship, witness, and obedience. Without its occurrence there cannot be either accurate knowledge of the will of God nor the determination to do that holy will. In fact, there can be no dynamic, personal knowledge of God without this gracious action of God. At the same time God's action promotes the response of believers. In this response there is, as we shall see, an important place for meditation and contemplation.

CHAPTER 3

Mercy and Faith

*R*enewal is through God's mercy. No other way exists by which we sinners can be prepared for fellowship and communion with our Lord Jesus Christ either in this sinful age or in the glorious age to come. Further, God's mercy also includes the gift of faith, whereby we not only appreciate but also receive his mercy and enter personally into his covenant of grace. Only by faith can there be authentic personal knowing and experiencing of the God of mercy.

RIGHTEOUS BY FAITH

Virtually all serious students of the letter to Rome agree that Paul intended to supply in 1:16–17 a careful summary of the essence of both his message and the contents of the letter.

> I am not ashamed of the gospel, because it is the power of God for the salvation of everyone who believes: first for the Jew, then for the Gentile. For in the gospel a righteousness from God is revealed, a righteousness that

is by faith from first to last, just as it is written: "The righteous will live by faith."

Here we find two major themes of the letter—faith and righteousness.

As a verb ("to believe") or noun ("faith"), believing the gospel has already been mentioned (1:5, 8, 12) and will become prominent (especially in 3:21–5:21; 9–11; 12:3, 6; and 14:1, 2, 22–23). In contrast, righteousness is first mentioned here in 1:17; however, like faith it often later appears as a noun or in verbal form (especially in chapters 3, 4, 5, 9, and 10).

Let us now examine in detail 1:16–17, taking each phrase/clause in order. This will serve to make clear the mercy of God, which is his righteousness.

I am not ashamed of the gospel—Probably Paul has in mind the saying of Jesus: "If anyone is ashamed of me and my words in this adulterous and sinful generation, the Son of Man will be ashamed of him when he comes in his Father's glory with the holy angels" (Mark 8:38). He joins other apostles and all the churches in asserting that he is confident the message concerning Jesus as Messiah and Lord is certainly good news/gospel for the whole world. Having carefully considered and meditated upon this message he is bold to declare his utter confidence in it.

because it is the power of God—The gospel is the power of God in terms of illuminating, converting, transforming, forgiving, sanctifying, saving, and glorifying sinners. This is the power of the Holy Spirit in human lives, made available because of the exalted Lord Jesus, who died for our sins and rose for our justification.

for the salvation—Salvation is deliverance from final destruction at the Last Judgment at the end of this age; therefore, it is also preservation and protection from now until then. Believers are to be wholly saved from sin and fully saved into the life of the age to come. Thus, in the present, salvation is experienced now in anticipation of its fullness in the presence of the Lord in glory, in the age to come.

of everyone who believes—Paul deliberately uses the present tense in order to point not only to the initial act of faith (believing the gospel) but also the continuing centrality of faith in the Christian life. For faith is the point of access for the saving power of God into everyone—whether Jew or Gentile, female or male, slave or free. And while faith is a human activity and attitude, it is also a gift of God, for it is inspired and energized by the Holy Spirit.

first for the Jew and then for the Gentile—Paul was a Jew who believed that Jesus was both the Jewish Messiah/Christ and the universal Lord/Savior. Though he was the apostle to the non-Jews (11:13; 15:16), he did not neglect his fellow Jews (see chapters 9–11). His missionary strategy was to go first to the Jewish synagogue and meet there the God-fearing Gentiles, through whom he went on to preach to other Gentiles.

for in the gospel a righteousness from God is revealed— In the West, due to the legacy of Roman law, we tend to think of righteousness/justice as an absolute ethical norm against which any particular claim or duty may be measured and judged. Here it is most likely that Paul is thinking not as a Roman but as a Jew who has been fully immersed in the thought of the Old Testament. Here God is presented as being righteous and providing righteousness because he is the faithful God of the covenant. He fulfills all the obligations that he as initiator of the covenant placed upon himself with respect to his chosen partners. Thus he acts righteously when he saves, protects, guides, and sustains his covenant people. (See for this meaning Isa. 45:8, 21; 46:13; 51:5, 6, 8; 62:1–2; 63:1, 7 and Pss. 31:1; 35:24; 51:14; 65:5.)

Righteousness points to a relationship established and maintained by God himself. In a covenant it is the infinitely stronger partner taking responsibility for the weaker partner. Thus, in the Gospel God declares that he is both placing in a new covenant with himself and then taking care of all who have faith, be they Jew or Gentile. Sinners who believe are declared to be in a right relationship with God, their Creator, Judge, and Redeemer. The weak and helpless who look humbly to God are brought under the gracious protection of the One who is strong. Forgiveness is offered in the present and total acquittal at the Last Judgment at the end of the world.

Paul declares that the righteousness of God is being revealed (present tense). In the preaching of the Gospel, God is actually revealing what previously has been hidden (known only in part in Israel) and what will be made fully known at the coming of the Lord Jesus Christ in glory. Yet what is now revealed is more than sufficient for redemption and salvation.

by faith from first to last—To translate the Greek (*ek pisteos eis pistin*) in this way is to see here a special emphasis on "by faith alone." This is one possible translation. Another, which I prefer, is "from [God's] faithfulness to [man's] faith." The virtue of this rendering is that it equates God's righteousness with his covenant faithfulness and unites this divine attitude and activity with the act of believing the gospel.

just as it is written—The quotation that follows is from Habakkuk 2:4. This serves as a proof text to provide the initial support from God's written Word for the great theme of justification by faith. Paul makes use of and adapts the Greek Septuagint, which literally translated is "the righteous out of my faith[fulness] shall live." His own Greek literally translated is "the righteous out of faith/faithfulness shall live." The point is surely clear. As covenant partners with God, human beings begin and continue by and in faith/trust. They are righteous in so far as they are made by God to be his covenant partners. Their righteousness is thus wholly dependent upon his. They are declared to be righteous solely and only because of his covenant faithfulness and righteousness.

From this brief study of Romans 1:16–17 it is possible to claim that justification by faith means entering and being sustained in a right relationship with God on the basis of believing the Good News from God concerning Jesus Christ. In this message is the announcement of a gift of righteousness. This is a right relationship through and in Jesus Christ with the righteous and faithful God within his covenant of grace, which begins now and continues into the age to come.

Justification is thus a major aspect of the mercy of God to undeserving guilty sinners (as Rom. 1:18–3:20 will demonstrate).

OLD TESTAMENT BACKGROUND

Paul's teaching on righteousness is developed from the Old Testament by the guidance of the Holy Spirit as the apostle reflects upon the saving work of the Lord Jesus. In the Law and the Prophets we find that to call God righteous is not to speak of the internal character of God. Rather, it is to speak of his attitude toward and relationship with Israel, his covenant people. Having freely chosen and adopted them, he always acts rightly toward them, sending them blessing or judgment, according to the terms of his gracious covenant.

"You are always righteous, O Lord," confessed Jeremiah (12:1). However, because by nature God is full of mercy and grace, his righteousness will include, Isaiah prophesied, the sending of his great salvation to his people, even though they break his covenant and do not deserve mercy. In fact salvation becomes a synonym for righteousness: "I am bringing my righteousness near, it is not far away; and my salvation will not be delayed. I will grant salvation to Zion, my splendor to Israel" (46:13). Paul therefore developed the theme of God's righteousness becoming God's own provision of salvation for the world.

For Israelites as covenant partners, righteousness refers to being in and maintaining a right relationship with the Lord their God. When viewed in the strictest terms and by the highest standards, the truth of the matter is that Israel as a people was not righteous: "All have turned aside, they have together become corrupt; there is no one who does good, not even one" (Pss. 14:3; 53:3; cited by Paul in Rom. 3:10–12). However, individual Israelites did faithfully seek to fulfill their covenant obligations to the Lord their God and to fellow Israelites, and they are called "righteous" (e.g., Pss. 33:1;

119:121; 146:8) as they do so by faith. We have to describe this as a relative righteousness, for when the full extent of the heart, mind, and will is open before God, the real truth is that "no one living is righteous before you" (Ps. 143:2).

Not only did the prophets look forward to the display of God's righteousness as salvation for Israel, but they also spoke of a future anointed servant of the Lord (Messiah) of the lineage of King David, who would lead his people Israel into God's salvation. In describing the future Messiah, the word "righteous" is often used or implied. For example, in Isaiah 11 the future descendant of David is described as being the one upon whom the Spirit of the Lord will rest, and

> He will not judge by what he sees with his eyes,
> or decide by what he hears with his ears;
> but with righteousness he will judge the needy,
> with justice he will give decisions for the poor of the
> earth.
> He will strike the earth with the rod of his mouth;
> with the breath of his lips he will slay the wicked.
> Righteousness will be his belt
> and faithfulness the sash around his waist (vv. 3–5).

By his life of faith and obedience, by his sacrifice of atonement and his resurrection from the dead, Jesus as Messiah brought God's righteousness and salvation to all who believe and trust in him.

ROMAN CATHOLIC/PROTESTANT

It is common knowledge that between Roman Catholics and Protestants a major division of interpretation concerning justification has existed. On the one side, Roman Catholic theologians have taught that to be justified means to be made righteous. According to this view, justification is seen as a process begun with the infusion of grace at baptism and completed before entry into heaven (through the cleansing experience of martyrdom or purgatory). Included in the process is the gift of forgiveness so that Christians may be said to be forgiven (and constantly being forgiven) sinners who are being made righteous through their reception of the grace of God in Word and Sacrament.

In contrast, on the other side, Protestants have always insisted that justification is a declaration by God the Father that for Christ's sake a believing sinner is accounted as righteous. His sins are forgiven, and he is adopted into the family of God and of the new covenant. Thus, a Christian is no more righteous at the end of his life than when he first believed, for he is always accounted righteous because of the righteousness of Christ. At the Last Judgment he will be judged righteous for Christ's sake. Yet there ought to be a growth toward maturity of faith and love in the Christian's life. This process is usually called sanctification and is deepened through Word and Sacrament.

It would seem that both systems of doctrine have been the means of helping believers to grow in holiness and toward maturity in faith, hope, and love for God and care for fellow human beings. Thus, there have been and are what we call "saints" exhibiting the grace and virtues of Jesus Christ in each tradition.

However, the old debate between whether "to justify" means either "to *make* righteous" or "to *count* righteous" may be judged to be somewhat obsolete if righteousness is taken to be what is explained above. That is, if divine righteousness is the activity of the covenant Lord on behalf of his unequal and weak partner (the sinful human being), then there is a real sense in which "to justify" includes both the declaration of being in the right (in a right relationship within the covenant of grace) and the subsequent process of making righteous (growing in covenant faithfulness). Yet if this interpretation be admitted, the emphasis is certainly upon the gracious activity of God in placing the believing sinner within the covenant and thereby declaring him to be righteous. The subsequent life within the covenant whereby the God of the covenant makes his inferior and sinful partner like himself actually follows from this even though it is a necessary part of it.

Further, to take "righteousness" to mean the activity of the covenant God admitting and supporting his unequal and often disobedient partner also makes it easier to resolve the old technical question as to whether "the righteousness of/from God" is a subjective or objective genitive: that is, does it mean "an activity of God" (subjective genitive) or "a gift bestowed by God" (objective genitive)? The NIV takes it as a gift bestowed by God while the RSV takes it as an activity of God. The best way is to take it to include both. On the basis of the activity of God a gift is bestowed. The believing sinner by God's activity is given the gift of membership in the covenant of grace. Such activity and such a gift are of divine mercy.

WHAT IS FAITH?

For Paul, to believe or to have faith is the necessary human response to God's mercy, which is proclaimed in the gospel, taught in the church, and experienced within the covenant of grace. Yet for the apostle, faith is also a gift of God in that it is created in the human heart by the mercy of God ("for it is by grace you have been saved, through faith—and this not from yourselves, it is a gift of God . . ." [Eph. 2:8]).

Such faith has three aspects or elements. It is to believe as true certain facts concerning Jesus Christ, e.g., that he died for our sins and rose from the dead for our justification. Also, it is to trust in and commit oneself to Jesus Christ as the only Lord, the One who alone brings sinners to the Father. Finally, it is to know God in the sense of having experience of God as the living Lord. Such experience comes to believing sinners in a variety of forms and ways; but however the experience comes, it is necessary in order for faith truly to be living faith.

The Christian life begins in faith and continues in faith, and without faith there is no genuine Christian living and activity. Faith is necessary to true theology: "I believe in order that I may understand" is a basic presupposition for doing theology. Further, faith is necessary to the true knowledge of God. There can be no genuine meditation upon God's truth and no contemplation of God in his mercy and grace without faith. Faith is the appointed channel and means whereby God places sinners in his covenant of grace and keeps them there in covenant faithfulness.

FAITH IN CHRIST

The classic passage in Romans where Paul states the relationship of righteousness, faith, and the sacrificial death of Jesus Christ is 3:21–26:

> But now a righteousness from God, apart from law, has been made known, to which the Law and the Prophets testify. This righteousness from God comes through faith in Jesus Christ to all who believe. There is no difference, for all have sinned and fall short of the glory of God, and are justified freely by his grace through the redemption that came by Christ Jesus. God presented him as a sacrifice of atonement, through faith in his blood. He did this to demonstrate his justice, because in his forbearance he had left the sins committed beforehand unpunished—he did it to demonstrate his justice at the present time, so as to be just and the one who justifies those who have faith in Jesus.

We must now look at this statement more closely in order to ascertain Paul's mind. As we do so we note that in this brief paragraph Paul uses the word *dikaiosunē* and its cognates seven times ["righteousness" (twice), "just" (once), "justice" (twice), "justify" (twice)]. Also, he uses *pistis* ("faith") twice and *pisteuo* ("to believe") twice.

> *But now . . . apart from law*—A new era has dawned and a new covenant is in place: and this has happened apart from and outside the ethnic, national, and religious parameters of Judaism.

a righteousness from God . . . has been made known—
God has revealed himself as the God of mercy, saving
action, and covenant faithfulness. The use of the perfect
tense ("has been made known") indicates that a decisive
event (i.e., the death and resurrection of Jesus, the
Christ) has taken place and that through this same Jesus
God's righteousness is known.

*to which the Law and the Prophets testify—*Paul sum-
mons the Law of Moses and the prophets of Israel as
witnesses. The content of their writings pointed to the
coming of the Messiah and the revelation of God's
righteousness and salvation in him to those who believe
in him (see Romans 4 and 9–11 where Paul fills out this
theme).

*this righteousness from God comes through faith in Jesus
Christ to all who believe—*God's merciful action on
behalf of those to whom he commits himself is freely
made available but only to those who wholeheartedly
believe in Jesus Christ. That is, God's righteousness
comes to practical, experiential expression in human
lives through faith in Jesus Christ rather than through
any fulfilling of mere ritualistic requirements. It is
significant that Christians are called believers ("all who
believe") here just as they are in the Acts of the Apostles
(2:44; 4:32; 5:14). Thus faith in Jesus Christ is the
distinguishing feature of all who are admitted to the
covenant of grace in and by the righteousness of God.

*there is no difference, for all have sinned and fall short of
the glory of God—*Both Jews and Gentiles are included
in this statement, for all people, with or without the Law
of Moses, have broken God's commandments and failed
to live as his obedient creatures who reflect his glory.
Therefore, all people are in need of God's righteousness
and salvation.

*and are justified freely by his grace—*The present tense
(*dikaioumenoi*) points to the time between the decisive
event of the death/resurrection of Jesus and the final
judgment at the end of the age. During this time frame
God is righteous as he places in the covenant of grace all
who believe in Jesus Christ. Such mercy is truly an
undeserved gift and proceeds from the compassionate
nature of God toward sinners.

through the redemption that came by Christ Jesus—In the Old Testament God is known as the Redeemer of Israel, particularly in the Exodus from Egypt (Deut. 7:8; 9:26; 15:15). The death/resurrection of Jesus is the new Exodus in and through which believing sinners are set free from the guilt and power of sin. They are set free in order that they may serve God as his covenant partners under the lordship of Christ, awaiting the final redemption of their bodies (Rom. 8:23).

God presented him as a sacrifice of atonement, through faith in his blood—Here Paul has in mind the sacrificial system of the Jewish temple. To fulfill God's requirement and thereby receive from God forgiveness and cleansing, the high priest on behalf of the whole people offered a sacrifice in the temple on the Day of Atonement (Lev. 16). To inaugurate the new covenant of grace God himself presented Jesus, the Messiah, as the atoning sacrifice for the sins of the world. By faith in this Jesus, who shed his blood for our sins and then rose from the dead for our justification, we receive God's righteousness and become members of the new covenant. Our sins are forgiven and we are promised acquittal at the Last Judgment.

he did this to demonstrate his justice, because in his forbearance he had left the sins committed beforehand unpunished—God provided a sacrifice for sins that more than fulfilled the conditions he had laid down in the old covenant with Israel. This atoning sacrifice, having been offered by the incarnate Son of God, is sufficient for sins committed both before and after it was offered.

he did it to demonstrate his justice at the present time, so as to be just and the one who justifies those who have faith in Jesus—Again Paul emphasizes the value of the sacrificial death of Jesus, for it shows that God is truly the God of the covenant who more than fulfills the obligations he has to his covenant partners. In fact by the death of Jesus the terms of the old covenant were both fulfilled and enlarged so as to admit into God's covenant (now new) those who believe in Jesus as Messiah and Lord.

To summarize: Faith is not just believing in God; it is believing and trusting in Jesus Christ in and by whom God is revealed as the God of salvation, redemption, and righteousness. By faith the believer is united with Jesus Christ and made a member of the new covenant. This faith is always at the very center of Christian experience and living, and thus from and through faith come the knowledge and service of God, the worship and obedience of God in daily life.

ACQUITTED IN GOD'S HEAVENLY COURT

At the end of Romans 8, Paul expresses his theology in a moving and powerful way. Here is part of what he wrote:

> If God is for us, who can be against us? He who did not spare his own Son, but gave him up for us all—how will he not also, along with him, graciously give us all things? Who will bring any charge against those whom God has chosen? It is God who justifies. Who is he that condemns? Christ Jesus, who died—more than that, who was raised to life—is at the right hand of God and is also interceding for us (vv. 31–34).

Here Paul brings together the atoning death of the Son of God, the benefits of the covenant of grace for those who are united to the Son, and the full and complete justification of believing sinners before God through Jesus Christ, who not only died and was exalted into heaven but actually intercedes there for the members of the new covenant. We shall examine only what he says about justification.

The "God who justifies" is in the present tense, and this serves to remind readers that justification from the perspective of the believer is not a once-and-for-all event. It has a beginning, a continuance, and an ending. Paul rejoices that in God's heavenly court no witnesses come forward to testify against those whom God has chosen. There can be no witnesses with damaging evidence since Christ has offered his sacrifice of atonement and has been exalted in heaven;

thereby he has closed the mouths of all accusers. From the day believers trust in him until they stand before God the Judge at the Last Judgment, they stand acquitted in God's holy court.

Paul underlines this truth by referring to the presence and continuing activity of the exalted Lord Jesus at the right hand of the Father. He is there not only as Lord of lords but also as the High Priest, as the Intercessor whose intercessions keep his faithful disciples in the covenant of grace while they continue their struggle on earth against the world, the flesh, and the devil. Their acquittal, which is sure, becomes final when in their redeemed, immortalized, and resurrected bodies they are placed everlastingly with Christ in the eternal kingdom of God.

NOT BY WORKS

Referring to his own Jewish people Paul declared that "they pursued [righteousness] not by faith but as if it were by works" (9:32). What did he mean by "as if it were by works"? Paul probably was not thinking of the earning of merit before God by doing good deeds for needy people along with required religious duties in home, synagogue, and temple. Rather, he had in mind the confidence placed by Jews in certain external aspects of their religion, and particularly those that related to their distinctive identity as "the people of the covenant." Thus, we are to think of those activities and customs that proclaimed their Jewishness, their non-Gentile-ness. These "works" gave them the sense of being a special people—a people to be judged worthy by their God because in celebrating their distinctiveness, they believed they honored the Lord their God.

JUSTIFICATION IN THE GOSPELS

The gracious justification of sinners by God is also taught in the Gospels, particularly in the parable told by

Jesus of the tax collector and Pharisee who went up to the temple to pray (Luke 18:9–14). The penitent tax collector who prayed, "God be merciful," went home "justified," said Jesus. Why? Because he knew himself to be an unworthy sinner and he looked only to the promises of God to be merciful to sinners. He was declared by Jesus to be in the covenant, in a right relationship with God.

God is righteous; his covenant partners, though sinful, are also to be righteous. Thus, the call to be just/righteous is a constant theme in the Gospels, especially that of Matthew. Jesus is portrayed as often rejecting the apparent righteousness of the Jewish religious leaders for it is incomplete, even hypocritical. Further, it is only external, having to do with outward performance of duties and not involving the custody of the heart and mind. In solemn words Jesus spoke to them, saying, "Woe to you, teachers of the law and Pharisees, you hypocrites! You are like whitewashed tombs, which look beautiful on the outside but on the inside are full of dead men's bones and everything unclean. In the same way, on the outside you appear to people as righteous but on the inside you are full of hypocrisy and wickedness" (Matt. 23:27–28). Though they seemed to be in a right relationship with the law of God, they were in fact breaking it in their hearts.

Jesus expected his disciples to aim high. "Seek . . . first the kingdom of God, and his righteousness" (Matt. 6:33, KJV); "Blessed are those who hunger and thirst for righteousness" (Matt. 5:6); and "unless your righteousness surpasses that of the Pharisees and the teachers of the law, you will certainly not enter the kingdom of heaven" (Matt. 5:20). In fact the Sermon on the Mount in Matthew and the Sermon on the Plain in Luke provide a full account of what it means to be righteous, to do righteousness and/or justice, and thereby to walk humbly with God. And the portrayal of final judgment by Christ at the end of the age in the vision of the Son of Man separating the sheep and goats (Matt. 25:31–46) clearly teaches that the righteousness of those who inherit the kingdom of God will be one that is found in attitude and action. ". . . whatever you did for one of the least of these brothers of mine, you did for me," (v. 40) Jesus will say to those who have freely loved the needy in righteous behavior.

Following the judgment by the Son of Man, God will establish righteousness as the characteristic of the new age, which is the fulfillment of the kingdom of God. "Then the righteous will shine like the sun in the kingdom of their Father" (Matt. 13:43). At the present time those who are declared righteous are to live righteously, longing for the perfect righteousness of the kingdom of heaven.

CHAPTER 4

Maturity in Faith

*T*hrough the mercy of God maturity in faith is that to which believers are to aspire. For not only does God declare his covenant partners to be righteous in his heavenly court, but he also provides all the necessary grace whereby they are able to make progress in the way of holiness toward practical maturity in faith and faithfulness. This alone is the way into the future glory of God in the age to come.

THE MERCY OF GOD

The apostle never tires of extolling and rejoicing in the mercy and grace of the heavenly Father. He seems unable to cease to mention the divine act of the justification of sinners. For example, he writes, "Therefore, since we have been justified through faith, we have peace with God through our Lord Jesus Christ, through whom we have gained access by faith into this grace in which we now stand" (Rom. 5:1–2). To this gracious act of placing believing sinners in the new covenant he unites the further work of God keeping them there by his Spirit and through his faithfulness. He states,

"There is now no condemnation for those who are in Christ Jesus, because through Christ Jesus the law of the Spirit of life set me free from the law of sin and death" (8:1–2), and ". . . God has poured out his love into our hearts by the Holy Spirit, whom he has given us" (5:5).

In fact Paul is confident that the Holy Spirit actually dwells in the hearts of those who believe in the Lord Jesus. How he refers to the Spirit is instructive. In quick succession he calls him "the Spirit of God" (8:9), "the Spirit of Christ" (8:9), and "the Spirit of him who raised Jesus from the dead" (8:11). Further, he adds, as an equivalent phrase "Christ in you" (8:10). Apparently Paul is teaching that the risen and exalted Lord Jesus Christ is now experienced in and through the Spirit, the Spirit who is the Spirit of creation and prophecy (Gen. 1:1ff.; 1 Peter 1:11). We are not to think that the Spirit and Christ are one and the same; rather, the "Spirit indwelling" and "Christ in you" are synonymous. Thus the lordship of Jesus Christ over his own is exercised by the presence and activity of the Spirit in their lives. On earth now Jesus is known only through the Spirit (who, according to John 14–16 is his *Paraklētos*, the One called alongside).

Later, in writing to Colossae, Paul spoke of the revelation of the mystery long hidden (see chapter six for a discussion of "mystery") and identified this with "Christ in you." "To them God has chosen to make known among the Gentiles the glorious riches of this mystery, which is Christ in you, the hope of glory" (1:27). The Spirit indwelling the believer is the guarantee that what Christ achieved by his cross and resurrection is being brought into the very center of the believer's life. What God planned before all ages is being personally experienced by each believer in the present, in anticipation of the fuller experience of the world to come.

Therefore, the Spirit indwelling the believer is one way of defining what is a true Christian. To this Paul would add that the Christian is a person who both has the Spirit and is led by the Spirit. Conduct and lifestyle inspired by the indwelling Spirit are necessary to the proper definition of a Christian. But not only does the Spirit inspire holy living, he also provides internal assurance of one's being a child of God and as such of having an intimate relationship with the heavenly Father.

Paul wrote, ". . . you received the Spirit of sonship. And by him we cry, '*Abba*, Father.' The Spirit himself testifies with our spirit that we are God's children" (Rom. 8:15–16). The verb *krazein* points to an intense or loud cry, a cry of sheer joy and confidence in God, the Savior and Father. The Aramaic word *Abba* implies an intimate sense of sonship, a privileged access to the Father who is always there to hear the prayers of his children. The Spirit indwelling the heart communicates directly with the human spirit—the uncreated Spirit bears witness and the created spirit cries out. Here we must recognize an emotional intensity that truly belongs to authentic Christian spirituality.

This intensity is also present in Paul's description of the way in which the Spirit causes prayer to arise from within the human heart—prayer that is "with groans that words cannot express" (8:26). The believer who in Christ belongs to the age to come actually lives day by day in the present evil age. It is living in this tension of belonging to Christ in heaven and being in the world of space and time that is the basis for the need for divine assistance in prayer to God. Here the Spirit is helping the believer not to reach the heights of ecstatic rapture, but to be able to speak to God in ways appropriate for a faithful member of the new covenant. "We do not know what we ought to pray for, but the Spirit himself intercedes for us with groans that words cannot express" (8:26).

Thus, for Paul the grace of God is nothing less than the Spirit's indwelling the believer and being the inspirer of righteous praying and living, holy fruit (Gal. 5:22–23) and spiritual gifts (Rom. 12:6–8). In the Mosaic covenant the Spirit visited specific individuals from time to time to empower them for divine duties, but in the new covenant the Spirit actually dwells in the soul. Or, as Paul prayed elsewhere, "that Christ may dwell in your hearts through faith" (Eph. 3:17). God dwells with his believing people—with his believing and faithful people. From the human side the key is faith—faith that is faithful, faith that works by love, and faith that is obedient.

COVENANTAL DUTIES OF GOD'S CHILDREN

As the apostle celebrates the mercies of God he also places before his readers the duties of those who are the recipients of these mercies. These covenantal responsibilities may be viewed in terms of duties toward God, fellow believers, and the world. Of course to make rigid demarcations would be to go beyond Paul's presentation, for these duties overlap and interconnect. This admitted, the threefold description is helpful.

A. *Duties toward the world.* These include a right attitude toward the state (13:1ff.), the loving of neighbor and the blessing of enemies and those who maltreat and persecute believers (12:14–21), the confession of Christ as Lord (10:5–10), and the participation in the evangelization of the world (15:30–33).

B. *Duties within the fellowship of Christians.* From chapter 12 through to the end of the letter, Paul gives a variety of exhortations, principles of action, and suggestions that are designed to lead the congregation at Rome to live together truly as the people of the new covenant, as those in whom the Spirit dwells and as members of the one body of Christ.

C. *Duties toward God.* All duties toward the world and the church are of course duties toward God also, for they are to be performed out of love for him. But in terms of direct relationship to God, Paul has much to say of duty toward the Father, toward Christ Jesus the Lord, and toward the Spirit.

We need to ponder the third area, for it lies at the heart of the major concern of this book.

First of all, in exploring duties to God, there is the always present duty of "[believing] in your heart that God raised [Jesus] from the dead" and "[confessing] with your mouth, 'Jesus is Lord'" (10:5–11). The faith by which the believer first believes is to grow and expand, to intensify and deepen as it encounters and receives more of the grace of God (8:28ff.).

Second, from the confession that Jesus is Lord flows the committing and handing over to him of one's life so that believers are, in Paul's terms, "slaves to righteousness" (6:18) and "slaves of God" (6:22, but see the entire passage, 6:15–23). "Offer yourselves to God," he wrote, "as those who have been brought from death to life; and offer the parts of your body to him as instruments of righteousness" (6:13).

In the third place, there is the responsibility of recognizing that one is indwelt by the Spirit of Christ and of becoming sensitive to his promptings, guiding, helping, and leading (8:5ff.). "We have an obligation . . . by the Spirit [to] put to death the misdeeds of the body . . ." and to express the inner life of the Spirit in outward behavior (8:12–13).

Fourth, there is the duty to maintain a right relationship with God as his covenant partner. This includes not only believing and trusting him, being submitted to him, and following the leading of his Spirit but also rejoicing in his salvation, hoping for the glory that shall be revealed, and loving God as the God who first loved us (5:1ff.).

Paul saw all these duties with others as flowing from and within faith and at the same time as the fruit of grace. As he wrote elsewhere, ". . . continue to work out your salvation with fear and trembling, for it is God who works in you to will and to act according to his good purpose" (Phil. 2:12–13).

THE MIND OF CHRIST

There is no growth toward maturity of faith without that renewal Paul calls for in Romans 12:1–2, which we examined in chapter two. Ceasing to be conformed to the world and being transformed by the renewing of the mind is essential to progress on the path toward holiness and eternal life (6:22). Where there is a renewed mind, covenant duties are performed willingly for the glory of God.

A renewed mind can develop only where the Spirit indwells the heart and soul. Paul contrasts the renewed and the sinful mind when he writes, "Those who live according to the sinful nature have their minds set on what that nature desires; but those who live in accordance with the Spirit have their minds set on what the Spirit desires. The mind of sinful man is death, but the mind controlled by the Spirit is life and peace" (8:5–7).

The apostle is describing the general orientation and disposition of human nature and uses the verb *phronein*. This means not only to think but also to have a settled way of understanding and a settled attitude. Paul describes two opposed attitudes flowing from two different principles — either the reason, imagination, feelings, and will are engaged with and absorbed by things and matters that proceed from self-interest, or they are taken up with the service of the living God, doing what he desires.

Further, as Paul made clear in chapters 1–3, the condition of human beings without the grace of God is death—that is, separation from God at the end of the age and also as lacking vital communion with God now. In contrast, those in whom the Spirit dwells have life—they know God and have fellowship with him as his covenant partners. They also have peace, which is both the peace with God brought by the divine act of justification and the internal peace or tranquility of heart that the sense of being reconciled to God evokes in the soul. Thus, peace is the antithesis of the misery and alienation that sin creates in the human heart.

Of course in day-by-day experience Christians were not then (as they are not now) people who always and wholly take the side of the Spirit. They also sometimes take the side of their own human nature, which is not yet totally renewed; they also sometimes fall prey to temptation and commit sins. This is because they still belong to the present evil age and world (Rom. 5:12–21). As long as they are in the flesh with mortal bodies they cannot escape the reality of the power of sin. However, because they are reckoned by God the Father to be in Christ they belong to the future age of righteousness, which will dawn at the Second Coming of the Lord Jesus Christ and which is present now in and through the Spirit. They are on the road of faith toward maturity and perfection; they press on but have not reached the goal. They have within themselves the power of two ages—the present one and the one to come; thus, there is a certain tension in their existence between the "already" and the "not yet." Already believers experience the powers of the age to come, but not yet in fullness, for the best is yet to be.

It is in this tension that believers are called to fulfill their covenantal duties to God and to do so in the strength and with the guidance he supplies. It is here that we are to see the great importance of prayer, meditation, and contemplation. Prayer—meditative and contemplative prayer—is in a vital sense that channel of grace that makes effective the other means of grace. It is a divinely appointed lubricant to allow and to cause believers to enjoy fellowship with their God and from this to gain the necessary illumination, inspiration, and insight to do his will. At the center of such prayer is the contemplation of the exalted Lord Jesus Christ—as Paul himself provides evidence of so doing in Romans 8:31ff. He ends the chapter in this way: "I am convinced that neither death nor life, neither angels nor demons, neither the present nor the future, neither height nor depth, nor anything else in all creation, will be able to separate us from the love of God that is in Christ Jesus our Lord." (See chapter five.)

There is no maturity in faith and love where there is no contemplation of the invisible world of heaven, for there the

Lord Jesus sits at the right hand of the Father in glory, surrounded by the holy angels. In fact "faith is being sure of what we hope for and certain of what we do not see" (Heb. 11.1).

So it is not surprising to read Paul's exhortation to the church in Colossae: "Since, then, you have been raised with Christ, set your hearts on things above, where Christ is seated at the right hand of God. Set your minds on things above, not on earthly things. For you died, and your life is now hidden with Christ in God" (3:1–3). This call for heavenly mind-edness or contemplation on Christ in glory is accompanied also by a call to mortify sin: "Put to death, therefore, whatever belongs to your earthly nature: sexual immorality, impurity, lust, evil desires and greed, which is idolatry" (v. 5).

The putting to death of sinful desires is obviously for Paul inseparable from minding the things of the Spirit and contemplating the heavenly Lord. Likewise, in Romans 8 he also calls for mortification: "If by the Spirit you put to death the misdeeds of the body, you will live" (v. 13). In fact where there is mortification and heavenly mindedness it can be humbly claimed that "we . . . are being transformed into [Jesus'] likeness with ever-increasing glory, which comes from the Lord, who is the Spirit" (2 Cor. 3:18).

MATURITY OR PERFECTION?

Over the centuries there have been persistent calls in the church from both Roman Catholics and Protestants for Christians to aim for "perfection"—be it perfection in holiness or love, or both. Inspiring this call are the words of Jesus: "Be perfect . . . as your heavenly Father is perfect" (Matt. 5:48; cf. Matt. 19:21). The Greek word translated "perfect" is *teleios*.

We may claim that to be perfect is the state or condition of being completed or finished without any defect or excess. Yet the perfection of the red rose in bloom is a different perfection from that of a hand-carved chair; and the perfection of the mathematical formula is a different perfection from that of the four-leaf clover. Further, the perfection of God himself is a different perfection from that attainable by his creation. If God possesses absolute perfection as the eternal and infinite Lord, then the perfection reached by human beings (made in his image, after his likeness) must be in comparison a relative perfection.

Therefore, in talking about Christian perfection, which has been the title of many books and sermons over the centuries, we are talking about relative perfection. As the Lord is holy love in his eternal and infinite Being, so we are to be filled with that holy love in our souls to the fullest extent human creatures are capable of being filled, both now and later in heaven. At the same time we must remember that our capability of being filled will be extended in the age to come when, free of mortal bodies, we are living in immortal, glorious bodies and, free from the stain and pull of sin, we are living only in the presence of God himself.

We find that the word "perfect" (translating *teleios*) occurs more often in the letters of Paul in the King James Version than it does in modern translations. They use other words instead—"mature," "complete," and "whole." Such words help to make clear that Paul saw perfection in two different but complementary ways.

First of all, there is a perfection of human beings as creatures that is final and absolute, but it belongs only to the future kingdom of God in heaven. Putting this in terms of his personal pilgrimage, Paul wrote, "One thing I do: Forgetting what is behind and straining toward what is ahead, I press on toward the goal to win the prize for which God has called me heavenward in Christ Jesus" (Phil. 3:13–14). The picture in Paul's mind is that of the runner who knows how distracting a backward glance can be and who exerts every effort to press forward with the race. He seeks to run without swerving, for he hastens to the goal, to Jesus Christ himself who is seated at the right hand of the Father in heaven. He seeks to attain to the resurrection of the dead, to fullness of life in an immortal body with a renewed heart, mind, and will.

Paul also spoke of this future perfection in his great hymn of love (1 Cor. 13). "When perfection comes, the imperfect disappears," he wrote (v. 13). He continued, "Now we see but a poor reflection as in a mirror; then we shall see [God in Christ] face to face. Now I know in part; then I shall know fully, even as I am fully known [by God]" (v. 12). To see God will be to experience everlastingly the love of God (v. 13).

In the second place, there is a perfection that is relative when compared with the perfection that shall be in the age to come. This relative perfection may be called "maturity." There is no doubt that Paul saw his work as an apostle not only to make converts for Jesus Christ but to lead the converts on (both as individuals and as societies of believers) to maturity of faith, hope, and love. Not a maturity that has a final form but a maturity that has a potential for growth toward God as long as the believer is alive.

Paul likened the growth within the Christian life to human growth from infancy through childhood to adulthood. True spiritual and moral adulthood is (relative) perfection. This is clear from his use of the word *teleios* in 1 Corinthians. First of all in 2:6 he claims that the apostles "speak a message of wisdom among the mature," but the members of the church in Corinth were not yet ready for that wisdom. They were not spiritual and mature but worldly (3:1ff.). Then in 14:20 he urges them in this manner: "Brothers, stop thinking like children. In regard to evil be infants, but in your thinking be adults." They were to be mature and adult in their thinking. It is one thing to be childlike and another to be childish. The Corinthians were not employing their minds in the worship and service of Christ as they ought.

If we turn to the letter to Colossae we meet this relative perfection in several contexts. Paul claimed, "We proclaim

[Christ], admonishing and teaching everyone with all wisdom, so that we may present everyone perfect in Christ. To this end I labor, struggling with all his energy, which so powerfully works in me" (1:28–29). Here we can take *teleios* ("perfect") to refer to the ultimate perfection, but in the context it is better translated/understood in terms of true maturity. Paul exerted all his energy and looked to God for help in order to present his converts to Christ as mature believers (in contrast to immature children).

The next example from Colossians is very much a corporate perfection/maturity. "Therefore, as God's chosen people, holy and dearly loved, clothe yourselves with compassion, kindness, humility, gentleness and patience. . . . And over all these virtues put on love, which binds them all together in perfect unity" (3:12, 14). Here the word is *teleiotēs* ("perfect harmony"). The maturity of a Christian fellowship is seen when its members live together harmoniously by exercising the virtues, of which the most important is love.

The final example in Colossians occurs in Paul's description of the prayers of Epaphras (see 1:7). "Epaphras, who is one of you and a servant of Christ Jesus, sends greetings. He is always wrestling in prayer for you, that you may stand firm in all the will of God, mature and fully assured" (4:12). Here *teleios* ("mature") means obeying God's will in practical living day by day so that they can stand firm against heresy and persecution and temptation. His prayer that they will be "fully assured" may mean "have clear convictions as to the essence of the gospel" or "filled with a profound sense of God's grace and will."

The perfection that was the goal of Paul's ministry was one that admitted of continuous growth; however, it was possible for him to say that some churches and some individual converts had actually reached a stage that could be called "maturity" as compared with others who were as yet children in their Christian faith and duties. Yet that maturity, which by the grace of God some had reached, was not the top of the mountain but a staging post on the way up.

There is no spiritual complacency in Paul's doctrine of maturity. His own testimony is that of always needing to run the race, to fight the good fight, to press on toward the mark, to set his mind on things above, to reach out toward Christ in glory, and to win Christ's commendation. Whatever depths of love he has experienced, there is more to be experienced; and whatever heights of union with God he has reached, there are yet greater heights to climb toward. And what applies to Paul himself applies also to every believing Christian. Though each Christian has his or her own personality and personal relationship with God, the general call is for him or her a *particular* call. There are no barriers of age, intellect, race, or sex, for all are called to the highest and deepest experience of the living God.

We shall discover that this is the teaching not only of Augustine but also of both Teresa of Avila and John Owen as well as of Eastern Orthodox teachers in their presentations of prayer and holiness.

CHAPTER 5

Faith and Meditation

The letters written by the apostle Paul and preserved in the New Testament confirm what we learn from the Acts of the Apostles concerning him. He was a careful and committed student of the Jewish Bible, our Old Testament, knowing it in both Hebrew and Greek. The letters also reveal that he did more than read and study the Law and the Prophets. As a Christian, he prayed the Psalms in and through Christ and meditated not only on their content but also on the whole of the Old Testament. He also pondered the facts concerning Jesus Christ, which he learned either by direct revelation or through the apostles and disciples. Further, as one who desired full communion with God within the new covenant, he contemplated the glory of God in the face of the exalted Lord Jesus Christ.

PAUL AS MEDITATOR

To search in Paul's writings for a method of meditation is to search in vain. All that needs to be said has been said, Paul would say, by the psalmist in Psalm 1:1–3.

Blessed is the man
  who does not walk in the counsel of the wicked
or stand in the way of sinners
  or sit in the seat of mockers.
But his delight is in the law of the Lord,
  and on his law he meditates day and night.
He is like a tree planted by streams of water,
  which yields its fruit in season
and whose leaf does not wither.
  Whatever he does prospers.

The art of meditation for the Jews was to read aloud the appointed portion of sacred Scripture over and over again in order to impress its content/truth deeply on the heart/mind as well as to commit it to memory. The word was to be tasted, seen, and heard so that it could enter fully into the whole man.

Paul would certainly have studied, repeated, prayed over, and memorized the Law and the Prophets. Beginning in his stay in Arabia after his encounter with the risen Lord on the road to Damascus (Gal. 1:17), the apostle developed the art of reading and meditating upon Scripture as a believer in Jesus Christ. No longer did he see the Scriptures as sacred documents waiting to be fulfilled, but he read them as already fulfilled through the incarnation, atonement, resurrection and exaltation of the Lord Jesus, the Messiah of Israel and the King of kings.

By the time he came to write the letter to Rome he had spent much time meditating upon the Scriptures (Old Testament) in the light of Jesus Christ and had developed a Christian interpretation of them. Thus the evidence that Paul was a meditator is to be seen in the result of that meditation—the contents of his letters. We shall look at several general themes and then examine specific verbs.

In the apostle's presentation of the righteousness of God, it is possible to see not only theological exposition based upon study but also evidence of the result of prayerful theological reflection and meditation. The theme is obviously something that gripped not only the mind but also the heart of Paul, and he presents it as being dynamic truth concerning the living God. It is probable that this theme originated in his meditation upon the righteousness of God as this is encountered in the prophetic literature of the Old Testament. In this prayerful study and reflection, pursued as a disciple of Jesus, he came to see that God's righteousness is the key to the power of the Gospel. For just as God's righteousness placed and maintained sinful Israel in the old covenant, so also the new, extended form of God's righteousness, made known and available through faith in Jesus Christ, places unworthy sinners in the new covenant of grace and maintains them there until their final acquittal at the Last Day—and this despite their unworthiness and weakness.

In contrast, the presentation of the presence and work of the Holy Spirit in the lives of believers (Rom. 8) points to meditation upon Christian experience—his own and that of his converts. Of course this is done within the tradition of teaching concerning Jesus Christ that he received from colleagues and from his own reflections upon the fulfillment of prophecies in the Old Testament (e.g., Jer. 31:31ff.) concerning the inward nature of the new covenant. Whatever be the precise origins of his study and meditation, we may say that the result is not cold dogma but warm and encouraging teaching on the presence and work within believers of the Spirit of God, who is also the Spirit of Christ.

Romans 9–11 are probably the most difficult chapters of the letter for modern people to appreciate since Paul is dealing with a problem there that is remote for most of us. However, a careful reading of these chapters will show that what Paul writes is obviously the result not of merely reading the Old Testament but of considering its contents carefully and prayerfully in the light of the person and work of Jesus, the Christ. He shows that there is more to the record of God's dealing with the patriarchs and their descendants than first meets the eye. For read in faith and with the mind of Christ, the books of the Law and the Prophets provide us with the inner history, the history within history, of God's covenant of grace, first established with Abraham. Further, the meditative posture of his mind is clearly seen in the way he ends chapter 11 with what may justly be called a hymn of adoration (vv. 33–36). Genuine meditation often raises the heart in praise to God, for the soul is lost in wonder, love, and praise. There is a close connection between biblical meditation and affective mysticism—as we shall see with Bernard of Clairvaux.

The evidence that Paul was committed to meditation is seen not only in the general contents of the letter but also in specific verbs. For example, the verb *logizesthai*, usually translated "to count" or "to reckon" appears in 3:28; 4:6; 6:11; and 14:14. It is a forceful verb denoting conviction that issues in practical action. In 6:11 believers are called to count or reckon themselves dead to sin and alive to God in Christ Jesus; this earthly reckoning answers to God's heavenly reckoning of them as righteous, members of his covenant of grace (3:28; 4:5).

What is involved in such reckoning by believers? Obviously, vital faith is one thing, the believing that Jesus died for them and that his sacrifice of atonement for sin at Calvary is the only basis of their being reckoned by God as righteous. Meditation is another: Believers are to look to the Lord Jesus, who died for them, and see themselves as dead to sin and alive unto God in and through him. Faith exercised in meditation upon the Lord Jesus has the effect of giving believers strength to live as God's righteous people in this present world (see chapter six for further comment on Romans 5:11).

In fact it could be said that meditation on the death and resurrection of Jesus by the believer is to be imitative of the activity of God in his reckoning/counting/crediting the believing sinner as righteous before him. God reckons to be true now what will be true in the future kingdom of God; he counts believing sinners as righteous ones now. In meditating upon the Lord Jesus, sinners believe that united to him in faith and by the Father's declaration they have actually died in/with Christ to sin, and have risen from sin/death into the new life of the kingdom of God. (In the same way it can be claimed that contemplation of God and his works by his obedient creatures is imitative of God's own contemplation of his creation: "God saw all that he had made, and it was very good" [Gen. 1:31]).

In 12:3 we find three verbs that point to specifically Christian thinking or meditation. "I say to every one of you: Do not think of yourself more highly [*huperphronein*] than you ought, but rather think [*phronein*] of yourself with sober judgment [*sophronein*], in accordance with the measure of faith God has given you." The verb *phronein* means to think or to form an opinion or to have an understanding, while *huperphronein* is an understanding or opinion that is proud and haughty. *Sophronein* is to think modestly, with discretion and care. Thus, Paul makes it clear that the type of thinking appropriate for the believer and in accordance with the measure of faith each one has from God is thinking that forms an understanding that is modest and discreet in humble submission to God in his self-revelation. Such thinking is what true meditation is all about; by it the mind is renewed, and through it the soul moves on to contemplation.

Perhaps it is to state the obvious to say that the character of meditation is determined by that upon which the mind works. It is possible to consider, ponder, and reflect upon subjects that are evil or that tend toward anxiety and depression. To meditate upon Jews as inferior and obnoxious people, as did Hitler and his supporters, is evil in every respect. This is certainly to cultivate the sinful mind. But to meditate upon one's own self so as to add to one's worries is also wrong. For example, if I have a pain in my chest and am waiting for the results of medical tests, I can meditate upon the possible diagnosis and thereby encourage fear of its consequences. This also is to serve the sinful self. In contrast Paul urged, "Whatever is true, whatever is noble, whatever is right, whatever is pure, whatever is lovely, whatever is admirable—if anything is excellent or praiseworthy—think about such things" (Phil 4:8).

OUR SITUATION

It is a long way from the spirituality of Paul, the converted Jew who became the apostle to non-Jews, to the situation in Western, secularist culture. In churches where the Bible has a prominent place, we are encouraged to study it carefully but are rarely told to meditate upon it in the style and spirit of Psalm 1. We need perhaps at this stage to think about the relationship of study and meditation.

Recently in a British theological college the external examiner required all students who were taking a unit in pastoral studies to write for him a meditation on one of several topics based on the life and teaching of our Lord, using passages from the Gospels. When he had collected all the papers and read them, he was very surprised. Apparently none of the students had offered to him a meditation. Instead they had provided what may be called exegetical and homiletical comments, treating the Bible either as an ancient document to be studied or as a source for sermonic material. They had failed to realize that meditation belongs to the category of prayer and that a written meditation is meant to be a record of an encounter with the Lord on the basis of having read, considered, and digested his Word.

The external examiner would probably have received similar results in other British theological colleges as well as in the average American theological seminary. Many students and ministers find it easier to use the Bible either academically or as a source on which to hang their sermonic material rather than as the originator of an encounter with God in prayer. And these attitudes seep through into the way in which members of Christian congregations come to view and use the sacred Scriptures.

Today, as we look on the shelves of Christian bookstores, we see a great variety and abundance of aids to assist in the reading and basic study of the Bible. Not only is a variety of translations of the Bible available, but the shelves are laden also with illustrated dictionaries, encyclopedias, lexicons, handbooks, guidebooks, and commentaries of varying shape and size.

Therefore, for those who are willing to make the effort to read the Bible with one or more of these aids at hand, it is possible over a period of time to gain an informed knowledge of the background and contents of the Scriptures. The extent and depth of knowledge and understanding will of course vary from person to person according to ability and the amount of time given to this basic study. The knowledge gained can be extremely useful in providing a general framework of understanding so that we better appreciate worship, sermons, and hymns as well as official church pronouncements on social and moral concerns. That knowledge will also be useful in helping us to work out our Christian vocation and duty in home, church, and society.

Personal study may proceed with the help of technical aids and also be extended by the use of daily Bible-reading programs as well as by participation in group Bible study. These usually seek to combine the study with some application to the present day and with suggestions for prayer. In fact, some Bible-study groups engage in prayer before and/or after their studies. Not a few people have "discovered" vital Christianity through such groups, for the warmth of the fellowship gives an extra dimension to the reading and hearing of the words of Scripture and thus helps to open the heart and mind to the love of God.

What is true at the basic or popular level of Bible study is also true at the higher levels—in the professional study of the sacred text. There is a vast amount of literature—greatly extended if you can read German—on the background, purpose, and contents of the books of the Bible. Those who are studying theology for a degree or diploma have access to all kinds of reference books, commentaries, and specialized articles and essays in journals and symposiums. The general purpose of all these publications is to help the scholarly reader of the Bible appreciate what the original author/editor of the book was seeking to communicate to the people of his day and time. It is, therefore, a "scientific" enterprise in search of the "literal" sense of the books that make up the Hebrew and Greek canons of Scripture.

Of course, the further you actually move away from the basic level of ordinary Bible reading/study, the more difficult it becomes to keep the study within a prayerful atmosphere and ethos. This is because Biblical Studies as an area of study in the modern university operates according to academic principles. Thus, as a subject it absorbs and reflects the general ethos of the university. This state of affairs is often confusing for a young person from a conservative Christian background (catholic or evangelical) as she or he begins a university career; it seems at first that the whole purpose of Bible study in the university or seminary is to take away one's "simple" faith. And some do lose their faith and study the Bible merely and only academically. Others learn to read the Bible in a critical and scientific manner, and then find it hard to use the Bible in a prayerful way.

I know from personal experience as well as from the candid admissions of friends who teach theology that the problem faced by new, devout students is, in varying degrees, a problem that remains for all scholars who want to be committed orthodox Christians as well as experts in modern biblical studies. Even as a medical doctor can become so fascinated with the disease and its cure that he forgets that the patient is a person with feelings, so a scholar of the Bible can be so absorbed by the study of text that he forgets the living God to whose self-revelation the text bears faithful witness. The separation of the scholarly pursuit from the devotional use of the Bible is not inevitable, but it is common. And because Christian professors and lecturers have not been able to work out a right or satisfactory resolution in their own lives, they find it difficult to give sound advice to their students. My own conviction is that, if there is a resolution of the problem, it will come only when the devotional use of the Bible—in prayer, meditation, and contemplation—has priority in personal experience, and thus establishes some kind of pervasive ethos in which to fit the different ethos generated by the study in the secular university.

These reflections and comments lead me on to make two claims, one negative and one positive. The first is that the God and Father of our Lord Jesus Christ does not expect or require all his children to study the Bible (in the academic sense); the second is that he does expect all his children prayerfully and in faith to meditate upon his revelation. This means that all Christians need to gain knowledge of (and preferably to memorize classic portions of) the Scriptures, for it is in them that the unique record of God's revelation is to be found. To gain such knowledge means either constant reading or hearing the Scriptures, and it may well be that such reading/hearing is best done as a kind of low-level study using a dictionary/encyclopedia/commentary. Meditation, however, does not of necessity have to proceed from Bible reading or study. It can arise (and over the centuries often has) from a believing mind recalling the contents of the Bible or by hearing the Bible read. But whether it follows low-level study or is based upon the Scripture learned by heart, its purpose is to be a channel or means whereby we fulfill Paul's directive: "Let the word of Christ dwell in you richly" (Col. 3:16).

After careful observation and inquiry, I have come to the conclusion that the best way to introduce believers to the art of meditation upon Scripture is to adopt a modern form of

Hebrew meditation. It is to learn to read the sacred text slowly, prayerfully, and formatively—and preferably to read aloud. To speak of this reading as formative is to make a contrast with informative. Most of our reading—of newspapers, books, letters, and reports—is done quickly and in order to gain information for our own purposes (be they good or bad). We are, as it were, in the driving seat and go where we will in the reading and at our convenience and speed.

Formative reading is done in such a way as to allow the text to form us, to let God the Holy Spirit be in charge, and thus allow the Inspirer of Scripture to become for us its Illuminator so that its content (a little at a time) enters our souls. (I have described this approach in more detail in my *Meditating As a Christian*.) Such an approach is sometimes like the experience of a lover reading a letter from the beloved. She does not read merely for information but to be formed not only by what is obviously the meaning of the text but also by what lies deep in the phrases and clauses, even what lies between the words and the lines.

To learn the art of formative reading is to meditate. From this base it is possible to go on and to deepen or extend the formative reading by adopting one or another of the methods of meditation developed by both Roman Catholics and Protestants (especially the Puritans of Old and New England) to cause the content of the sacred text to enter mind and heart. These methods are often referred to as discursive, for they encourage the mind to look up and down and over the text for illumination and insight. Unless we base them today upon the art of formative reading, methods of meditation can so easily become formal and even barren. This said, we need to be aware that over the centuries many sincere people have benefited from them and found their affections (e.g., faith, hope, love, and reverence, etc.) raised toward God in prayer by using them.

There is another way of thinking about the entry of the Word of God through meditation into our souls, to live in mind, heart, and will. It is to think of its entry and inner life within us in terms of motherhood—even the unique motherhood of Mary, mother of Jesus, who prayed, "Be it unto me according to thy word" (Luke 1:38, KJV). Margaret Magdalen writes:

> If we compare our experience to that of motherhood, first comes the conceiving of the word. We nurture it within us, as a mother-to-be nurtures the new life within her womb. We mother it, protect it, foster and feed it, allowing it growing space. We listen to its heartbeat and its movements within, to what it is saying to us—indeed demanding of us and our obedience. And as we grow with it, changes take place in us. We find a new purpose in being, for we carry the word within. But that is not all, of course. Like Mary, at the appointed time, we bring it forth to the world, holding out the word of life that has power to save (*Jesus: Man of Prayer*, InterVarsity Press, 1987, 98).

We all need to pray, "Be it unto me according to thy word."

CONCLUSION

Bearing in mind what I have just said, I hope I will not be misunderstood when I say that it is not wise to read (and seek to put into practice) the ways of prayer described in such books as the anonymous late-medieval *The Cloud of Unknowing* or the sixteenth-century *The Dark Night of the Soul* by St. John of the Cross or *The Interior Castle* by his friend St. Teresa of Avila until one is well into the habit and discipline of meditation upon the Scriptures. These were all written primarily for monks and nuns and do not begin where most of us actually are. We need to climb a step or two up Jacob's ladder or get into the holy cloud (*Shekinah*) or cross the bridge into the interior castle before we read too much about (and, more so, begin to practice) the ascending and deepening degrees of contemplation or mystical prayer.

In fact, the beginnings of truly affective and contemplative prayer will arise naturally within disciplined and regular meditation for those who sincerely desire to commune with their God and love and praise him. A beginner will find Francis de Sales' *The Devout Life*, Martin Luther's *A Simple Way To Pray*, Richard Baxter's *The Saints' Everlasting Rest*, or Jonathan Edwards' *Personal Narrative* (quoted in chapter one) better introductions to meditation and contemplation than the books mentioned above. These lead the reader from the one to the other slowly and carefully.

It is not wise to be too theoretical about prayer, since it is a part of an interpersonal relationship. And each of us is different from the other. It is both an addressing of God our Father and a listening to the Word he speaks to us in and through the Lord Jesus by the Holy Spirit. Prayer follows the general pattern of a conversation between a subject and his or her king or of a child and his or her father. Meditation is like both the careful consideration of a proclamation or statute of the king and the loving study of a moving letter from a caring father. It includes a variety of thoughts and feelings as well as types of prayer (for example, thanksgiving, confession, petition), and is intended to lead on to deeper worship and adoration, praise and thanksgiving, petition and intercession, communion and fellowship. Further, meditation is a spiritual duty out of which we must never grow. In saying this, I am not saying that Christians are to stop there and not allow meditation to become affective mysticism and contemplation. Rather, I am saying that day by day we have in a sense to begin at the bottom of the ladder and ascend in faith and by God's grace toward the Lord Jesus Christ in glory.

CHAPTER 6

Faith and Contemplation

To insist that mysticism or contemplation is a necessary part of the total Christian life of prayer is to run into a major problem. This is because there are two major evaluations of Christian contemplation or mysticism, and they are opposed to each other. One belongs to the central, older tradition of scholarship in both Orthodoxy and Roman Catholicism, the Eastern and Western branches of the church. The other belongs to theories about the emergence of patristic dogma and spirituality held by certain influential European Protestant theologians. It is our task to look at each of these in order to make an evaluation.

First, however, we need to reflect upon the relation of meditation and contemplation and notice how Paul described the experience of God in the Christian life.

SIMILAR BUT DIFFERENT

Up to now I have used "meditation" and "contemplation" in such a way as to suggest that they point to related but different ways of approaching God through faith in Jesus Christ. Meditation normally leads on to contemplation.

If we turn to the older English dictionaries, we find that in ordinary usage meditation and contemplation have had little difference in meaning. Both point to the activity of the mind as it considers, reflects upon, and muses over some fact or object. Where there is a difference, "contemplation" is used in more of that situation where the mind is still and fixed upon an object to behold it, whereas "meditation" is used as more of the activity of the mind looking at something from various angles or perspectives. Thus, we could say that the verbs "to see" and "to behold" belong more naturally to contemplation while the verbs "to consider" and "to reflect upon" belong more naturally to meditation.

As far as I can tell, the terms "meditation" and "contemplation" have been used interchangeably in Protestant writing and spirituality. However, the distinction made above is often found, though it is rarely made into a formal distinction. For example, in what may be called a classic of English Protestant spirituality, *The Saints' Everlasting Rest* (1649), Richard Baxter teaches his readers how to meditate upon the Lord Jesus in heaven. In this book Baxter sometimes speaks of meditating and at other times of contemplating. The same may be said concerning John Owen, a contemporary of Baxter, to whom we turn in a later chapter, and of Jonathan Edwards, who was quoted in chapter one. In fact this interchangeable usage may be found almost universally in Protestant and Anglican writers.

However, if we turn to Roman Catholic literature, we find that from the sixteenth through the twentieth centuries a formal distinction is made between meditation (usually described as discursive meditation) and contemplation (usually equated with mysticism). Meditation, as part of mental prayer, is seen as the first step toward the deeper, personal knowledge of God that is contemplation. One finds a few exceptions to this trend. For example Ignatius Loyola, the founder of the Society of Jesus, uses contemplation in his *Spiritual Exercises* when he refers to the preliminary meditating and gazing upon Jesus as he is pictured through reflection upon and imaginative reconstruction of a Gospel story. But the formal distinction is found in such classics as Francis de Sales' *Introduction to the Devout Life* (1608) and the writings of Teresa of Avila, to whom we turn in a later chapter.

We also have to bear in mind that today both words are used in the context of non-Christian, Eastern spiritualities (not to be confused with Eastern Orthodoxy). There they have a very different meaning from that which they bear in both Catholic and Protestant spirituality. As used in these Eastern spiritualities, which regrettably are now found even within churches and certainly where the New Age movement is strong, meditation and contemplation point specifically and only to an inward journey into the depths of the soul to find unity with everything that is. There is no related outward journey in faith up to the right hand of the Father in heaven where the Lord Jesus is enthroned in glory. Therefore, we see that, while there may be some similarity in language and even in technique for becoming still and attentive, a great difference in doctrine and purpose exists between biblical, Christian meditation and contemplation on the one hand and Eastern or New Age meditation and contemplation on the other.

After careful thought and much discussion, I have adopted the distinction suggested above between meditation as the prayerful considering of and reflecting upon God's truth, and contemplation as the gazing upon, beholding, experiencing, and seeing by faith God through Jesus Christ. Thus, I have moved toward the classic patristic, Roman Catholic, and Greek Orthodox distinction without adopting a too formal approach. However, I must say that what is clear to me from the study of Protestant writers on meditation and prayer is that Protestants (especially the devotional writers of the seventeenth through the nineteenth centuries) generally include within what they call meditation that communion with God, delighting in God, and experiencing God that most Roman Catholics specifically place within contemplation and mysticism. This claim will become clearer as we look at the teaching of John Owen and Teresa of Avila. It has already been indicated through the quotation from Jonathan Edwards' *Personal Narrative*.

FROM MEDITATION TO CONTEMPLATION

If I had to choose only one short passage from Paul's letters to commend meditation that develops into contemplation and the practical obedience of faith in Christ, it would be Colossians 3:1–4; and if I had to choose one verse it would be Romans 6:11. "Count yourselves dead to sin but alive to God in Christ Jesus." We shall look first at Colossians and then return to Romans.

The short paragraph at the beginning of Colossians 3 is pregnant with suggestions for heavenly meditation and contemplation:

> Since, then, you have been raised with Christ, set your hearts on [better, "seek"] things above, where Christ is seated at the right hand of God. Set your minds on things above, not on earthly things. For you died, and your life is now hidden with Christ in God. When Christ, who is your life, appears, then you also will appear with him in glory (vv. 1–4).

Earlier Paul had written, "You died with Christ" (2:20); now he writes, "You have been raised with Christ." The verb, *sunēgerthēte*, is in the aorist tense, emphasizing that their resurrection with Christ is a past event. It is a fact. Thus, their death with Christ severed the links that bound them to the old order/age of sin and death; and their resurrection with him established a permanent link with the new heavenly order/age/creation. So they are to look upward in order to receive clear direction concerning their conduct—God's will for them.

What is above is the exalted Lord Jesus Christ who is seated at the right hand of the Father. (The imagery of Psalm 110 is used to convey the transcendent order of heaven.) Believers must seek (*zēteo*) this heavenly realm, for it is here, and here alone, that Christ is. And since Christ is supreme in the invisible, supernatural world, no spiritual powers of any kind can prevent believers who seek the Lord Jesus from finding him. This seeking is a form of meditation. It is the raising up of the mind/heart to God through prayerful reflection upon the exalted Lord Jesus as he is presented to us in Scripture.

Having sought and found the Lord Jesus Christ through prayerful study of the revelation concerning him in the New Testament, Christians are to set their minds upon him in that heavenly realm. They are to contemplate him in his glory as the reigning and the coming Lord; they are to ravish their minds by fixing them upon his excellencies and virtues, his offices (Prophet, Priest, and King), and his graces. And they are to adore him as God incarnate. This setting of the mind upon Jesus in his glory is not a merely intellectual gaze, for it is the gazing in delight and love.

Paul urges that this heavenly contemplation is both appropriate and necessary because their life in the new epoch is hidden with Christ in God. They have already (even though they still live on earth in mortal bodies) a heavenly life that will, at the Second Coming of Jesus to judge the living and the dead, be fully embodied in new, immortal, resurrection bodies. Contemplation unites believers consciously with that divine reality that is invisible and hidden with Christ— their everlasting life. From this gazing upon Christ, believers are renewed and strengthened to live for Christ in the world of sin and death until his return in glory.

We now turn to Romans 6:11 where the apostle makes use of the verb *logizesthai* in the imperative form to point to the duty of the believer. It is a verb of some intensity ("count with conviction"). Paul uses it in 3:28 to speak of God's counting, or reckoning, believers to be righteous before him through Jesus Christ. The fact that it is used by the apostle first of God's act and then of the believer's act reminds us that, in the covenant relationship, God often calls believers to do as creatures and in a creaturely way what their Creator himself does as God.

In the context of chapter 6 (not only verses 1–10 but also 10–23) the duty of counting with conviction involves at least the following:

A. A deepening conviction that Jesus Christ not only truly died but in his dying so dealt with the fact of sin and death as to make himself free of them and of the epoch/age in which sin and death have "ruled" (i.e., from Adam onward).

B. A deepening conviction that Jesus Christ was raised from the dead and by his resurrection brought into being the new creation, age, and epoch that will be fully revealed and known after his Second Coming to judge the present, Adamic epoch. Meanwhile the new epoch is known and experienced in the life of faith through the presence of the Holy Spirit (as chapter 8 makes very clear).

C. An intensifying faith commitment to the living, exalted Lord Jesus and thus to his death at Calvary as being the death that includes the death of all believers to the Adamic, evil age. By the death of Jesus, membership in the old epoch is cancelled for those who are united to him in faith. Though they live within it until their death, their first and everlasting membership is in the new age of which Christ is Lord.

D. An intensifying faith-commitment to the exalted Lord as the One who has conquered sin and death and who calls the believer to live unto God and not unto the old Adamic epoch. Further, to live unto God in hope of the resurrection of the body and the fullness of life in the age to come whose center is Christ himself.

E. A definite, wholehearted recognition that an integral part of the act of dying with Christ to the old epoch of sin and death is the actual act of believing/thinking/counting oneself dead. Thus to meditate upon the death, resurrection, and exaltation of the Lord Jesus is integral to Christian faith and maturity.

Therefore, when believers meditate in this manner and within this framework of faith, they are placing themselves truly and experientially in the covenant relationship as unworthy but faithful covenant partners. They find that their minds slowly drop into their hearts, and their hearts are set aflame by the truth of what they are considering. Then the flame sends the will into action to serve God practically in the duties of the covenant. Thus, consideration can and perhaps always ought to lead both to contemplation and practical Christianity that is centered on the Lord Jesus Christ, Mediator of the Covenant, enthroned in heaven.

PAUL, THE CONTEMPLATIVE

It would be unwise to separate too rigidly Paul's meditative prayer from his contemplation of God. Knowledge of the Lord Jesus Christ and of God the Father through Jesus and by the Holy Spirit is for Paul faith-knowledge. To ponder God's Word or work in faith is to find one's heart kindled in love for God and to experience a close communion with him. Though the apostle does not deal systematically with the experiential knowing of God in the contemplation of him, one finds many indications in the letter to Rome and in other letters that Paul both enjoyed this experience and commended it to others.

Take for example what Paul writes in Romans 5:1–5. He speaks of being at peace with God, of having access into a gracious relationship with God, of rejoicing now, even in suffering, in hope of the future glory of God, and of having the experience of God's love poured into the heart through the gift and presence of the indwelling Holy Spirit.

Let us explore two of these four themes. First of all, "access by faith into . . . grace" (v. 2). As the royal chamberlain led the suppliant into the presence of the king—a great and solemn privilege and experience—so the Lord Jesus has led those who believe in him into the presence of God, the Father Almighty. The verb "have gained" is in the perfect tense, and this points not only to an access in the past but also to the continuing validity of that access. Therefore, communion with God is always possible, for the way to the Father in and through Jesus Christ by faith is always open. The invisible world where God is known in contemplative prayer is always reachable, for the access in Christ is open to those who have believed and continue to believe the gospel.

In the second place, "God has poured out his love into our hearts by the Holy Spirit, whom he has given us" (v. 5). The verb "to pour" is in the perfect tense, suggesting that the pouring of the love of God is, as it were, in full flood and is thus more than sufficient for every receptive heart. In contrast the verb "to give" is in the aorist tense, reminding us that the gift of the Spirit came on the Day of Pentecost (Acts 2) to the church and is permanently with believers, keeping them as people who rejoice in hope of the glory of God. Contemplation of God arises from within faith-knowledge but is inspired and motivated by love, the love of God within the believing people of God.

Communion and friendship with God are real now in this sinful age and world, Paul insists, but they are only at the beginning of their full development. In the kingdom of God believers will experience a richer and greater knowledge of God as they live to see the glory of God in the face of Jesus Christ.

Nevertheless, from time to time, God in his gracious and sovereign love lifts the humble believer into a profound union of will with himself. Paul knew of such experiences ("visions and revelations," 2 Cor. 12:1) and gives a memorable account of one such in these words:

> Whether it was in the body or out of the body I do not know—God knows. And I know that this man— whether in the body or apart from the body I do not know, but God knows—was caught up to paradise. He heard inexpressible things, things that man is not permitted to tell.

However, to keep the apostle from pride concerning such revelatory experience, he was given "a thorn in [his] flesh" (2 Cor. 12.7). So he learned to confess, "When I am weak, then I am strong" (v. 10).

In weakness Paul knew the presence and power of the Spirit of Christ. In turning to the Lord Jesus he had come to know God in a way that was wholly impossible in his days as a Jew in Judaism. Writing to the church in Corinth, he described the new experience of the Lord in this way (2 Cor. 3:13–18):

> We are not like Moses, who would put a veil over his face to keep the Israelites from gazing at it while the radiance was fading away. But their minds were made dull, for to this day the same veil remains when the old covenant is read. It has not been removed, because only in Christ is it taken away. Even to this day when Moses is read, a veil covers their hearts. But whenever anyone turns to the Lord, the veil is taken away. Now the Lord is the Spirit, and where the Spirit of the Lord is, there is freedom. And we, who with unveiled faces all reflect the Lord's glory, are being transformed into his likeness with ever-increasing glory, which comes from the Lord, who is the Spirit.

This description makes the reader want to know more of that experience of God that comes when the veil is taken away. But words fail to express the glory of the Lord that is beheld in such a situation.

In general it is true to say that the writers of the New Testament are not interested in what we now call the psychology of religious experience. They pointed to the truth as given in the Gospel, taking for granted the experience associated with the truth. Therefore such familiar statements as "I have been crucified with Christ and I no longer live, but Christ lives in me" (Gal. 2:20) and "Christ in you, the hope of glory" (Col. 1:27) must be seen both as providing doctrine and pointing to experience of God in terms of a close union of will with the Lord Jesus Christ. The same must also be claimed for Paul's teaching in Ephesians 5:25–32 of the relationship of Christ and his Church as that of Bridegroom and Bride, bound together in a unity that is the spiritual equivalent of "one flesh." There is mystical union of the Lord Jesus and his beloved that has to be experienced to be truly appreciated.

Within the relationship of Bride to Bridegroom and the members of the body to their Head is what may be called an ecclesial mysticism that is union with Christ in suffering. Paul wrote, "Now I rejoice in what was suffered for you, and I fill up in my flesh what is still lacking in regard to Christ's afflictions, for the sake of his body, which is the church" (Col. 1:24). The apostle made similar statements in 2 Corinthians 4–6. Obviously the suffering on behalf of Christ and the Gospel is not to fill up the suffering of Calvary, for that suffering is completed, and it was once and forever. Rather, suffering on behalf of Christ is to suffer with Christ now in his mission through his body in the world (the church) as he brings people to the Father through himself, the Mediator. Open conflict exists between the Gospel and the wisdom of God in a crucified Savior on the one hand and the world, the flesh, and the devil on the other. Obviously, an important aspect of experiential knowing of God or of mystical communion with God is in our suffering for Christ's sake. Many saints and martyrs, known and unknown, have proved this in their own lives.

Within the letter to Rome, what Paul teaches about the

presence and activity of the indwelling Holy Spirit (or Spirit of Christ or Christ himself) in chapter 8 must surely also point to a profound experience of God known in the midst of life, be it in peace or in suffering. Even as Jesus himself addressed the Father as "Abba," so believers by the Spirit also address God, the holy Father, as "Abba"; further, the witness of the Spirit of Christ with the inmost spirits of believers must also point to a mystical experience of God that is not available through any other means. And the ecclesial mystical union with Christ in suffering is clearly taught in this same chapter: "We are heirs—heirs of God and co-heirs with Christ, if indeed we share in his sufferings in order that we may also share in his glory" (v. 17). And in the next verse he writes, "I consider that our present sufferings are not worth comparing with the glory that will be revealed in us."

As commended by Paul, contemplation may provisionally be defined as a beholding/viewing/gazing upon God in his self-revelation and his reconciliation of the world in Jesus Christ. Humble souls penetrate these truths in order to be in closer communion with God. In practice this means contemplating of Jesus Christ, the exalted Lord, as the One in and by whom God is known. And God often meets the soul that is thus contemplating by making his presence real and known. Sometimes the contemplation is most real and vivid in suffering.

In the technical terms for prayer used by Roman Catholic theologians, the general form of contemplation I see commended as normal for believers in Paul's letters may be called acquired contemplation or the prayer of acquired recollection or the prayer of simplicity or the prayer of loving attention. As such it is usually seen as the bridge between meditative and affective prayer and the ever-enlarging possibilities of mystical prayer.

Such contemplation is understood as a simple, loving gaze upon some divine object, whether of God himself or one of his perfections; on Christ or on one of his offices; or on some other Christian truth. The movement of the mind in search of truth has ceased. In its place is a simple intellectual gaze that is motivated by love. The affections generated by meditation are here focused in the gazing upon Truth, and this brings inner delight to the soul—joy, peace, love. Thus, when the affections are uppermost and the will is directed into union with God . . . that is mystical experience. It can last a long or short time and is capable of endless expansion by the grace of God.

I like the following description of the beginnings of contemplative prayer given by the French bishop Jacques Bossuet (1627–1704):

> We should accustom ourselves to nourish our soul by a simple and loving look on God and on Jesus Christ: and for this we must disengage it gently from reasoning, discourse, and the multitude of affections, in order to keep it in simplicity, regard and attention, and so bring it nearer and nearer to God. The soul should not stay in meditation, for by its fidelity in mortification and recollection, it ordinarily receives a purer and more intimate prayer, which may be called "prayer of simplicity," consisting in a simple looking or loving attention to . . . God himself. The soul quitting reasoning, uses sweet contemplation, which keeps it peaceful, attentive, and receptive of any divine impressions the Holy Spirit may communicate (*A Short and Easy Way of Making the Prayer of Faith*, n.d., 3).

Perhaps this basic contemplative prayer, which may by God's grace develop into a more profound and enlarged experience of God in faith and knowledge, is that which is captured by Paul's prayer wish as expressed in Ephesians 3:14–21:

> For this reason I kneel before the Father, from whom his whole family in heaven and on earth derives its name. I pray that out of his glorious riches he may strengthen you with power through his Spirit in your inner being, so that Christ may dwell in your hearts through faith. And I pray that you, being rooted and established in love, may have power, together with all

the saints, to grasp how wide and long and high and deep is the love of Christ, and to know this love that surpasses knowledge—that you may be filled to the measure of all the fullness of God.

Now to him who is able to do immeasurably more than all we ask or imagine, according to his power that is at work within us, to him be glory in the church and in Christ Jesus throughout all generations, for ever and ever! Amen.

Such a doxology provides a fine example of the effect on the soul of contemplation—it is uplifted in adoration and praise. A soul thus moved is the more likely to be the soul that engages in the practical obedience of faith in daily duties.

THE PROTESTANT CHARGE

From a line of European theologians beginning with Albrecht Ritschl (1822–1889) and including Adolf Harnack (1851–1930), Emil Brunner (1889–1966), Anders Nygren (1890–1970), and Karl Barth (1886–1968), we have heard the charge that contemplation or mysticism as understood and specifically practiced by monks and nuns in patristic, medieval, and modern times is not authentically Christian prayer. True prayer, they assert, is prophetic prayer—praise, thanksgiving, confession, intercession, and petition. The reasons for this charge are varied, and those who have made it have not always supplied the same reasons. It is possible, however, to summarize the content of the charge.

It is alleged that contemplation is a form of prayer that naturally belongs to monism—the doctrine that there is only one reality. The multiplicity of realities that we experience is only appearance. Everything is one: the one is known and experienced as one in prayer or Eastern-style meditation. This type of mysticism became part of the piety of monks in the fifth century through their adapting for Christian use the doctrine and practice of contemplation that one finds in the teaching of Neoplatonist writers (e.g., Plotinus). Harnack, who advanced the thesis that classic dogma (as in the Nicene and Athanasian Creeds) is the fruit of the growth of the Gospel in Hellenistic soil and a movement away from biblical teaching, also regarded mysticism as the result of the hellenizing of Christian prayer. The goal of "hellenized" prayer, Harnack claimed, was union with God, being lost to self and absorbed into deity. This experience was sought at the expense of biblical, Christian prayer—thanksgiving, petition, and intercession, for example.

Therefore, one must conclude that contemplation or mysticism is to be judged a regression to that form of prayer found also in Eastern religions where the goal likewise is union in the depths of one's being with true reality or "God." Here the "I" merges with the "One." Contemplation, therefore, is a primitive form of prayer found in religions whose worldview is either pantheistic or monistic.

Scholars, usually but not always of a liberal viewpoint and apparently without serious investigation, have easily accepted the charge that some have forsaken the biblical pattern of prayer. The reason for this acceptance is not easy to determine, but it probably includes the following.

First of all, since the charge has been made by scholars of great learning such as Ritschl and Harnack, others have tended to accept their judgment uncritically.

In the second place, Christian mysticism has adopted words and phrases that were also used by philosophers in their teachings about the ascent of the soul into God as well as by teachers in the so-called mystery religions. We note, however, that to use the same words in no way necessarily implies that in the new context they mean the same thing.

In the third place, critics have misunderstood what some Christian mystics have meant by "union with God." Where the mystics have intended to speak only of the union of human will with the divine will, detractors have inferred a union of essence as well. Undoubtedly, the language used by mystics in their efforts to convey that which is beyond words has often been filled with hyperbole and paradox, not to mention metaphor, simile, and dialectical tension. But this is what we should expect since God as experienced in the soul is indescribable—even beyond the eloquence of the Spanish poet and mystic, St. John of the Cross.

Further, we see in the great mystics' non-mystical writings and in their activities a commitment to Christian theism and their acceptance of the profound difference and distinction between the Creator and his creatures. In fact, mystical writers often make clear that the union with God is a union of will, not of nature.

In his exposition of the mystical union of Christ and his church, which he based on Song of Songs, St. Bernard of Clairvaux wrote:

> "He who is joined to God is one spirit." The union between God and man is not a unity, at least if compared with the unique and sovereign unity of Father and Son. For how can there be unity where there is plurality of natures and difference of substances? The union of God and man is brought about not by confusion of natures but by agreement of wills (*Canticles*, lxxi, 5).

Fourth, contemplative prayer and mysticism have been traditionally associated with the devotional life of monks and nuns. Since Protestants have judged the monastic life to be contrary to biblical faith and practice, there has been an underlying tendency throughout Protestant history to question that which was seen as the high point of the prayer of celibate monks and nuns. Even great Protestant scholars have not been free of this doubt and questioning.

In the fifth place, the writings of mystics on contemplation make use of the Bible in ways that were well understood in the medieval period but are little appreciated now. Mystics loved, for example, to use the Song of Songs as a portrayal of the love of Christ for his bride, the church, and, further, his love for each member of the church—thus the experience of mystical union of love known in contemplative prayer. Though they did not deny the basic commonsense meaning of the text, they saw through it to a deeper spiritual meaning.

Finally, mystical writings are usually only about contemplation and nothing else. Therefore they give the impression that contemplation is the only really valid or worthwhile form of prayer and that others are merely secondary or preparatory. We must bear in mind, however, that the majority of those who wrote these books were members of communities where they had a full round of daily services that included the reading of Scripture, the celebration of Holy Communion, and the praising, thanking, interceding, and petitioning God through formal prayers as well as private prayer.

These considerations are not an answer to the charge that contemplation is not genuine Christian prayer, but they do help to place it in context. Several Roman Catholic scholars have sought to defend the authentically Christian character of contemplation against the charges of Ritschl and his successors. Of these the one who is most accessible to English readers is Louis Bouyer of Paris who has written a large number of books on Christian spirituality. I call attention to his *The Christian Mystery* (1990) and to his three-volume *History of Christian Spirituality* (1960–1976). However, I would also call attention to *The Origins of the Christian Mystical Tradition* (1981) by Andrew Louth and the studies he cites for further information and insight.

Bouyer's way of answering the charge is to set out the facts concerning contemplation as he sees and interprets them. He holds that this is the best way to meet a charge and a challenge that is based not upon scholarly, historical investigation but upon the application of certain prejudicial presuppositions to the reading of the primary texts. He has proved that European Protestant scholars were wrong in most of what they wrote in condemnation of mysticism. Of course, there is false and bad mysticism; at the same time there is genuine Christian mysticism and contemplation. It is only the latter that he and I defend.

FROM MYSTERY TO MYSTICAL

"The mystery of Christ, irreducible to any other, is the only true object of mysticism rightly so-called: Christian mysticism," wrote Bouyer. He is correct, but what did he mean?

"Mystery" (*mystērion*) occurs in the New Testament only twenty-seven times, and of these, twenty occur in the Pauline letters. Where the noun occurs in Paul's writings it is found with verbs that denote revelation or proclamation; thus the mystery is that which is revealed. (See Rom. 11:25; 16:25; 1 Cor. 2:1; 4:1; 13:2; 14:2; 15:51; Eph. 1:9; 3:3; 3:4; 3:9; 5:32; 6:19; Col. 1:26; 1:27; 2:2; 4:3; 2 Thess. 2:6; 1 Tim. 3:9; 3:16.) It is God's secret, a secret disclosed in the Gospel and revealed to the apostles.

At the center of what is revealed is the power of the cross of Christ to bring salvation to both believing Jew and Gentile. What God prepared in heaven and proclaimed in Old Testament prophecy has taken place in the death of the Messiah. The Cross is at the very center of God's saving purposes and of both cosmic and human history. From the work of Christ on the cross flow all the fruit of redemption—from cosmic regeneration and the summing up of all things, visible and invisible, in Christ through the creation of a covenant people of both Jews and Gentiles (as the bride of Christ) to the presence of the Spirit of Christ in each believer's soul.

This meaning of the word "mystery"—the interconnected Cross/Resurrection/Exaltation of Jesus Christ and all that flows from his revealing, reconciling, and redemptive work at Calvary—is found throughout the writings, liturgies, and prayers of the bishops and theologians of the patristic period.

The word "mystical" (*mystikos*) was first used in the

church in Alexandria in the period of Clement and Origen in the early third century to point to the real and true meaning of the Old Testament. The mystical meaning was that spiritual meaning that related the content of each book to the "mystery" of Christ—to the total saving work of God in Christ. To find the mystery concerning Christ in the Old Testament, the Alexandrian teachers developed what we call allegorical exegesis; thereby they came to the mystical or spiritual meaning. We find this usage throughout the patristic period. A biblical exegesis centered on the mystery of Christ was mystical exegesis. As St. Augustine later put it, "The New is in the Old concealed; the Old is by the New revealed." And this principle is well illustrated in his delightful *Commentary on the Psalms*.

In the second place, "mystical" came to mean those objects or aspects of the Christian faith that are invisible but nevertheless wholly real to faith. Thus we read of the "mystical Trinity/Triad," which is God, and of "mystical teaching concerning Jesus Christ," meaning his invisible deity.

A third meaning was that of "spiritual" in contrast to "carnal." Thus the kiss of peace in the Eucharist ought to be *mystical*—spiritual, not carnal.

A major development of meaning came when "mystical" was used of the spiritual presence and saving power of God in the Sacraments. We read of the "mystical bread," the "mystical sacrifice," the "mystical table," the "mystical action," and the "mystical Passover" with respect to the Eucharist and of "mystical regeneration" and "mystical water" with respect to baptism. The sacraments are *mystical* in that they contain or envelop the true "mystery" of Christ, the very mystery proclaimed by the Gospel and unveiled to the eyes of faith.

The final development, and that which most concerns us in this book, was to use "mystical" of the union with God known in worship and prayer. So phrases such as "mystical contemplation" begin to appear (e.g., in the writings of Gregory of Nyssa). By the sixth century in the very influential writings of Denys or Dionysius the Pseudo-Areopagite, "mystical" clearly refers to communion with God. The claim was that the Scriptures point to this experience and in contemplation the Christian comes to know that to which the Scriptures refer. Thus "mystical theology" (the title of a short but very important book by Denys) is not the academic study of spirituality but the *mystical* union with God the Father through God the Son by God the Holy Spirit. In contemplation the believer is said to enjoy the *mystical* knowledge of the living God, which is to know God experientially.

Thus to speak of mysticism is to speak of encounter with the *mystery*, which is Christ crucified, resurrected, exalted, and present now in the Spirit. Of course, genuine *mystical* experience is given only to those who have faith and also are faithful, for communion with God in Christ is the communion of *agape* (love) in humility. Therefore, it seems clear that as long as the *mystical* arises from the *mystery*, what we have is genuine Christian prayer that rises to the Father through the merits and mediation of the incarnate Son by the Holy Spirit and leads into union of wills.

Not only an allegorical and anagogical interpretation of Scripture developed in association with this understanding of the relation of *mystery* and *mystical*. Another development was the use of such themes as darkness and light in the experience of Moses and Jesus, and that of the nuptial love of the Bridegroom and bride (Christ and the believer) to convey the depth, height, length, and breadth of mystical experience of God in Christ. (For more detail see the section on Bernard in the next chapter as well as chapter ten, "The Orthodox Way.")

I realize that to claim all this concerning the mystery and mysticism is to make an evaluation of the patristic evidence that is wholly positive. Yet it is a claim that will stand careful investigation. However, it is also true that this development was set within a dependence upon one or more aspects of Neoplatonism (especially from the teaching of the influential Plotinus, born A.D. 204, who was a genuinely creative religious philosopher).

For example, it was widely held among the educated in the Roman world that contemplation was the ascent of the mind or soul from a lower level (this material world) to a higher or metaphysical level and that this ascent could not occur without the purification of the soul. Thus asceticism and contemplation belong together. Christians agreed that prayer is the ascent of the mind or soul, but they gave a very different account of the One to whom the ascent was made. Not to the Idea of the Good or to the Idea of the Beautiful but to the personal deity, who is the Father, the Son, and the Holy Spirit do the souls of the faithful rise. And they rise because of the love of God in Jesus Christ: God has descended that we might ascend!

Also the estimate of the human soul is different. For Plato and his disciples the soul is divine and achieves its destiny by rising in contemplation to realize its innate divinity and be assimilated into ultimate reality, the Ideas. In contrast, for Christians the soul is created by God out of nothing and never can be divine. Only by being incorporated into the human nature of the one Lord Jesus Christ, the God-Man, can the soul be united with God and, to use the language of Peter, be deified (2 Peter 1:4).

Further, we may note that in Neoplatonism the practice of virtue is for the purpose of assisting the ascent of the soul to God from the prison of the body. In Christian mysticism the practice of virtue is seen as the fruit of the indwelling Spirit of Christ and as the result of genuine fellowship and communion with God. Thus contemplation and action are held together in love, God's love for man and man's love for fellow human beings in and through God's love. Finally, within the Platonic tradition the mystic is the person, usually considered as a member of the intellectual elite, who has the leisure and inclination to engage in contemplation. In contrast, within the Christian tradition, because the mystery is to be preached to all and all are called to believe and receive Christ, mystical communion with him is also for all, according to the measure of their faith.

CONCLUSION

In surveying books on contemplative prayer, I have often noticed that they usually have nothing to say of petitionary and intercessory prayer. I suspect that a lot of people draw the conclusion from this fact that petitionary prayer and intercessory prayer are lesser grades of prayer. Such a conclusion is a false one. If we think of prayer as including adoration, praise, thanksgiving, confession of sins, petition, and intercession, then we may say that within genuine contemplation are adoration and praise and that confession and thanksgiving occur in the preparation for contemplation.

If so, where does asking God to do things fit in? Obviously petition and intercession are made in services of divine worship, and Christians offer such prayers at all times of the day and night. But what is the connection between contemplative and petitionary/intercessory prayer? If we look at the example of Jesus, especially as that is provided for us in the gospel of John, we see that Jesus makes requests of the heavenly Father in the context of his communion with him. John 17 contains what has been called the high priestly prayer of Jesus, and here we find vital communion with God and real requests on behalf of others. Then if we look at Paul's moving, prayerful concern for his fellow Jews (see Rom. 9:1–2; 10:1), it is obvious that his intercessions flow from his fellowship with God in Jesus Christ. Further, when Paul speaks of the intimate sense of belonging to God as his child, he also speaks of the indwelling Spirit interceding: "We do not know what we ought to pray for, but the Spirit himself intercedes for us with groans that words cannot express" (8:26).

As one reviews autobiographies and biographies of holy men and women, one finds that so often their pleading with God on behalf of others or for their own growth in wisdom and holiness arises within or as a result of their mystical, contemplative prayer. I have seen it in the lives of both Catherine of Siena and Catherine of Genoa as well as Bernard of Clairvaux, David Brainerd, and Samuel Rutherford. The fact that fervent supplication is intimately related to mystical communion serves to make the point that genuine contemplation is not an exercise in self-actualization or self-formation but is the communion of the creature with the Creator and of the Father with his child, leading to the practical loving of the neighbor. Genuine contemplation increases true virtue and compassion.

Contemplation without faith in the Lord and submission in love to him is not Christian contemplation. Religious ecstasy that is not the experience generated by the Spirit of Christ is not Christian mysticism. True contemplation and mysticism in the Christian faith are based on faith working through love in prayer, just as genuine good works are the fruit of faith working by love in practical Christianity.

Undoubtedly Paul lived daily knowing God experientially in what we have called contemplation and mysticism. His letters point in this direction. Further, his apostolic labors could have been so fruitful only because they were energized and sustained through vital communion with God.

What is true of the letters of Paul is also true in a related but different way of the gospel and letters of John. In these we find much that points to vital, personal knowing of God, of abiding in Christ in love, of the presence of the Spirit of Christ in the soul making Christ himself present, of feeding on Christ in our hearts by faith, and of participating in the glory of Christ.

CHAPTER 7

Mysticism—Augustine and St. Bernard

Augustine of Hippo is recognized on all sides as a great writer, thinker, and theologian. His *Confessions*, a classic so widely read that his personality has been one of the best known in history, testifies to his greatness. Born at Tagaste, near Carthage in North Africa in 354, he became a Christian in Milan in 386, returned to Africa, and became bishop of Hippo in 396. He died in 430. Augustine dominated the Western church by his pen, not by his deeds. He did not deny an empress and excommunicate an emperor, as did his old teacher, Ambrose of Milan. In his own town and monastery of Hippo in the midst of many varied tasks, he sought to know God and to write of that experience. He was no armchair theologian.

Of this great man, to whom both Roman Catholics and Protestants owe so much, Dom Cuthbert Butler has written:

> Augustine is for me the Prince of Mystics, uniting in himself, in a manner I do not find in any other, the two elements of mystical experience, viz., the most penetrating intellectual vision into things divine, and a love of God that was a consuming passion. He shines as a sun

in the firmament, shedding forth at once light and heat in the lustre of his intellect and the warmth of his religious emotion (*Western Mysticism*, 1926, 20).

But was he "the prince of mystics"? Certainly later mystics such as Teresa of Avila greatly valued his writings (see her *Life* in chapter nine). But I wonder whether it is better to present Augustine's spirituality as first of all intellectual, beginning with profound meditation upon Scripture and Christian doctrine but leading on to mystical contemplation, involving fervent desire for and love of the living God.

Certainly, Augustine was desirous of renewal—the renewal of the mind leading to the transformation of the person within the body of Christ. Of the renewal that we expounded in chapter two he wrote:

The renewal of which we speak is not effected in the single moment of return, like the renewal which takes place in baptism in a single moment through the remission of sins—none whatsoever remaining unremitted. But it is one thing to be relieved of fevers and another to regain health after the weakness which fevers have caused. It is one thing to withdraw a dart from the body, and another to heal by further treatment the wound which it has inflicted. So here, the cure's beginning is to remove the cause of the sickness; and that is done by the forgiveness of all sins. Its furtherance is the healing of the sickness itself, which takes effect by gradual progress in the renewal of the image. Both are displayed in one text of Psalm 103, where we read: "who shows mercy upon all thine infirmities" which happens in baptism; and, then, "who healeth all thy diseases" which is a matter of daily advances whereby the image is made new. Of this the apostle had spoken in plain terms: "If our outward man decays, yet is our inward man renewed from day to day" (2 Cor. 4:16), renewed . . . "in the knowledge of God" (Col. 3:10), that is in "righteousness and holiness of truth." He who is thus renewed by daily advancing in the knowledge of God, in righteousness and holiness of truth, is changing the direction of his love from the temporal to the eternal, from the visible to the intelligible, from the carnal to the spiritual; diligently endeavoring to curb and abate all lust for the one, and to bind himself in charity to the other. In which all his success depends on the divine aid; for it is the word of God that "without me, ye can do nothing" (John 15:5 [*On the Trinity*, xiv, 17.23]).

Here Augustine's spirituality is clearly set forth. Contemplation is a part of the daily advance in the knowledge of God.

MYSTICAL EXPERIENCES

Before he became a Christian, Augustine became a Neoplatonist. This was, by his own admission, a step on the road by which God was leading him into his confession of Jesus Christ as Lord. While a religious Neoplatonist who was in search of God, he had a mystical experience at Milan in 386. Here is his description of an attempted ascent of the mind to God, expressed in the language of Plotinus (the famous Neoplatonist religious philosopher):

Step by step was I led upwards, from bodies to the soul which perceives by means of the bodily senses; and thence to the soul's inward faculty, to which the bodily senses report external things, which is the limit of the intelligence of animals; and thence again to the reasoning faculty, to whose judgement is referred the knowledge received by the bodily senses. And when this power also within me found itself changeable, it lifted itself up to its own intelligence, and withdrew its thoughts from experience, abstracting itself from the contradictory throng of sense images, that it might find what that light was wherein it was bathed when it cried out that beyond all doubt the unchangeable is to be preferred to the changeable; whence also it knew That Unchangeable; and thus with the flash of one trembling glance it arrived at THAT WHICH IS . . . but I could not sustain my gaze, and my weakness being struck back, I was relegated to my ordinary experience, bearing with me but a loving memory and a longing for what I had, as it were, perceived the odour of, but was not yet able to feed upon (*Confessions*, trans. E. B. Pusey, vii.23).

We noted in chapter six that Neoplatonism was a system of intellectual contemplation. The soul was encouraged to leave the lower world of senses and return to the "Ground of Being," be united with this "One," and thus realize its true nature. In 386 Augustine sought to do just this. Yet there was more to Neoplatonism than the mysticism. Through reading the writings of Plotinus at Milan in 385–386 Augustine was enabled to reconcile the presence of evil in the created world with the doctrine of the omnipotence of God. Their insistence on the anhypostatic character of evil was of great help to him in his thinking about the nature (not the Being) of God.

On becoming a Christian Augustine did not cease to be a Neoplatonist. However, there is never any doubt that this philosophy is always the servant of Jesus Christ, never the other way around. It is Plato baptized into and enrolled in the service of Christ. Augustine's debt to Plato and the whole platonic tradition, particularly to the form in which it was expressed by Plotinus and Porphyry, is obvious and cannot be denied. Yet Plato and the Platonists had to be conformed to Christ for Augustine, for the Bible and the Creeds always came before the philosophy books.

Much the same may be said of Denys the Pseudo-Areopagite (the most successful pseudonymist in European literature), who used Neoplatonism in the service of Christianity in the late fifth century as Thomas Aquinas was to use Aristotelianism in the mid-thirteenth century. Although for Western Christians Denys is much more difficult to appreciate than is Augustine, they are best seen as complementary, providing an intellectual Christian mysticism that in its philosophical basis may be traced back through Plotinus to Plato. Where possible it is good to study both writers together.

The influence upon Augustine of Neoplatonism in terms

of method and outlook is obvious, for example, in his description of the vision at Ostia, a shared experience with his mother, Monica. It occurred soon after he had become a Christian:

> We were discoursing together alone, very sweetly, and we were enquiring between ourselves in the presence of the Truth, which Thou art, of what sort the eternal life of the saints was to be. With the lips of our souls we panted for the heavenly streams of Thy fountain, the fountain of life which is with Thee, that, sprinkled with that water to the measure of our capacity, we might attain some poor conception of that glorious theme. And as our converse drew to this conclusion, that the sweetest conceivable delight of sense in the brightest conceivable earthly sunshine was not to be compared, no, nor even named, with the happiness of that life, we soared with ardent longing towards the 'Self-same' [i.e., the unchanging God], we passed from stage to stage through all material things, through heaven itself, whence sun and moon and stars shed their radiance upon earth. And now we began a more inward ascent, by thinking and speaking and marvelling at Thy works. And so we came to our own minds, and we passed beyond them, that we might come unto the region of unfailing plenty, where Thou feedest Israel for ever with the food of truth. There Life is the wisdom by which all things come to be, both those that have been and those that are to be; and the Life itself never comes to be, but is as it was and shall be ever more, because in it is neither past nor future but present only, for it is eternal. And as we talked and yearned after it, we touched it—and hardly touched it—with the full beat [*toto ictu*] of our heart. And we sighed and left there impawned the firstfruits of the spirit, and we relapsed into articulate speech, where the word has beginning and ending (*Confessions* ix.23,24).

Here and in later descriptions of an ascent of his mind to God, Augustine reveals a difference between himself and later mystics such as Teresa of Avila and John of the Cross. They begin in prayer and they come to experience the living God through prayer. For Augustine contemplation is primarily an intellectual process, informed and lubricated by the warmth of love for God. It is the search for Something/ Someone, not subject to any change, that drives the soul to God, who is above all beings and being. The search requires great concentration of mind and will. However, the experience of God claimed by Augustine as the climax of the ascent of the mind to God is apparently of the same nature as that claimed by later Christian mystical writers as the fruit of their prayer. In their different routes they head in the same direction to the same living God.

Augustine began his *Confessions* with the statement: "Thou hast made us for Thyself, and our heart knows no rest until it may repose in Thee." Holy desire ought to characterize the life of the faithful Christian, and contemplation may be said to be an important aspect of this holy desire for God. In his commentary on Psalm 42:1 ("As the deer pants for streams of water, so my soul pants for you, O God"), Augustine provides a marvelous exposition of contemplation of God arising from within the desire for the living God. Does not man derive his being from his relationship with God, and if he is fallen away from God will he not be disordered and disoriented until he returns to his Creator who is now also his Redeemer? In the return to God a man comes to know himself as he seeks to know God—as Augustine often prayed, "O God, who art ever the same, let me know myself and let me know Thee," and as he often said, "I desire to know God and the soul." For while God is wholly transcendent as Creator of all, he is also immanent and omnipresent. And thus as the mind ascends to God in holy desire, the same God is known in the depth of the soul.

One of the most memorable passages in the *Confessions* is the point where Augustine explains that the mind longs for the truth, for reality, for joy that endures—for God himself. And he writes of his own experience of not finding the living God:

> Too late have I loved Thee, O Thou Beauty of ancient days, yet ever new! Too late I loved Thee! And behold thou wert within, and I outside, and there I searched for Thee; and I sought Thee outside and in my perversity fell upon those lovely things that Thou hast made. Thou wert with me, but I was not with Thee. Things held me far from Thee, which, unless they were in Thee, would not have been at all. Thou didst call and shout to me and burst open my deafness: and Thou didst send forth Thy beams and shine upon me and chase away my blindness: Thou didst breathe fragrance upon me, and I drew in my breath and do now pant for Thee: I tasted Thee and now hunger and thirst for Thee: Thou didst touch me and I have burned for Thy peace (X.xxvii).

Augustine longed to be satisified in his mind and in the depths of his soul, and nothing would satisfy him except a living knowledge and encounter with the God and Father of our Lord Jesus Christ.

The return of the soul to God in contemplation is a major theme of his mature meditation, *De Trinitate* (On the Trinity). After first establishing from Scripture what God has revealed of himself—that he is Three Persons, One God— Augustine seeks to understand what he believes. In doing this he moves to provide an outline of how the soul can come to contemplate the God in whom it believes. He expounds the soul's ascent to God in terms of the triad of *retentio* (the holding in mind of the truths of Scripture), *contemplatio* (contemplating God through them), and *dilectio* (delighting in the God who is contemplated). Thus the soul returns to God, not in one moment of supreme ecstasy, but in a long process of renewal that will never end in this mortal life. And the soul follows a way that has been disclosed to the mind by the light of the one living God who is a Trinity of Persons. In following the revealed way the soul finds that the God who is Trinity discloses himself to the one who seeks him. For God is not only majestically transcendent; he also dwells by the Holy Spirit in the soul of man.

THE TWO LIVES

The important place of contemplation for the believer is made obvious by Augustine's description of the Christian life in its two aspects of active and contemplative. In a well-known piece from his comments upon John's gospel he wrote:

> The Church knows two lives divinely preached and commended unto her: whereof the one is in faith, the other in "specie"; the one is in the time of pilgrimage, the other in eternity of abiding; the one is in labour, the other in rest; the one is on the way, the other in the true country; the one is in the work of action, the other in the reward of contemplation; the one turns away from evil and does good, the other has no evil from which to turn away, and has great good to enjoy; the one wars with the foe, the other reigns without a foe; the one is strong in things adverse, the other has no sense of aught adverse; the one bridles the lusts of the flesh, the other is given up to the joys of the spirit; the one is anxious with the care of getting the victory, the other in the peace of victory is without care; the one is helped in temptations, the other, without any temptations, rejoices in the Helper Himself; the one assists the needy, the other is where it finds none needy; the one pardons the sins of others that its own sins may be pardoned, the other suffers nothing that it can pardon, nor does anything that calls for pardon; the one is scourged with evil that it be not lifted up with good things, the other through so great fullness of grace is without any evil, so that without temptation of pride it cleaves to the Supreme Good; the one discerns between good and evil, the other sees things which are only good; therefore the one is good, but still in miseries; the other is better and in beatitude (*Commentary on John*, cxxiv.5).

It is clear from this compelling statement that the full, contemplative life belongs to heaven and the glorious age to come.

In a sermon on the account of Jesus' visit to the home of Martha and Mary (Luke 10:38ff.), Augustine developed the symbolism of the two aspects of the Christian life, the active and the contemplative, from the action and attitudes of the two sisters:

> In these two women, both pleasing to the Lord, two lives were prefigured: the present and the future, the laborious and the quiet, the troublous and the happy, the temporal and the eternal. Both are praiseworthy; but the one is laborious, the other leisured. What Martha was doing, there we are; what Mary, that we hope for. While in this life how much can we have of Mary's part? For even now we do somewhat of her work, when removed from businesses and laying aside our ordinary cares. Inasmuch as we do thus, we are like Mary (*Sermon* civ. 4).

So the beginning of the life of contemplation is both possible and appropriate here in this world. In his great work, *On the Trinity*, he wrote of Martha and Mary in these words:

> Jesus Christ will bring those who believe to the contemplation of God, where is the end of all good actions, and everlasting rest, and joy that never will be taken from us. A similitude of this joy Mary prefigured, sitting at the feet of the Lord, and intent on His words; resting, that is, from all action, and intent on the truth in such wise as this life is capable of, whereby she prefigured what is to be in eternity. For while her sister, Martha, was occupied about things that had to be done, good indeed and useful, but destined to pass away when rest succeeds them, she was resting on the word of the Lord. And when Martha complained, He said, not that what she was doing was a bad part, but that Mary's was the best, which should not be taken away. For that which lies in ministering to want, when want is no more, is taken away. And abiding rest is the reward of a transient good work. In that contemplation God will be all in all; because nought else will be sought from Him, but it will suffice to be illumined by Him and to enjoy Him (i.20).

So this Christian life on earth in the midst of want is inevitably and necessarily a mixed life—active and contemplative.

Space and time has to be made by all for the contemplative, for that is "the better part." Of course Christians will differ in their ability to contemplate, but all are called to be as Mary was and to be attentive to the word of the Lord and adore him who speaks that word. "Let them choose for themselves the better part: let them devote themselves to the word of God; let them yearn for the sweetness of doctrine; let them occupy themselves with the knowledge that leads to salvation" (*Sermon* civ.2). It is in contemplation of the Lord that God renews within those who so pray his image and likeness, which has been seriously marred by sin. For man becomes like God through participating in him through contemplation. Such participation is in and through the Lord Jesus who is himself the true image of God. Spiritual mindedness is beholding the glory of God in the face of Jesus Christ, the Lord.

BERNARD OF CLAIRVAUX

Bernard (1090–1153), a Cistercian monk, founded and became abbot of Clairvaux. From there he traveled over Western Europe and engaged in a ceaseless round of activities of an ecclesiastical and political nature. Nevertheless he is remembered more as a contemplative than an activist. However, we perhaps can understand his contemplative spirituality, which speaks directly to the heart, only if we picture him preaching passionately to men, calling them to join in the Crusade to rid the Holy Land of the Muslim occupying forces. One finds a relationship between the way he prayed and the way he preached.

Like his mentor, Augustine, his writings have influenced Protestants as well as Roman Catholics. However, he was not a Neoplatonist and his contemplation is very much the contemplation of the heart and is thus more obviously affective than is Augustine's.

Bernard distinguished between meditation (or consideration) and contemplation in his book, *On Consideration,* addressed to his friend Pope Eugenius III:

> Contemplation is concerned with the certainty of things, consideration with their investigation. Accordingly contemplation may be defined as the soul's true and certain intuition of a thing, or as the unhesitating apprehension of truth. Consideration is thought earnestly directed to investigation, or the application of the mind searching for the truth (ii.5).

Further, in one of his sermons on the Song of Songs he distinguished between two types of contemplation, of intellect and of heart. "There are two kinds of transport (*excessus*) in holy contemplation: the one in the intellect, the other in the heart (*affectus*); the one in light, the other in fervour; the one in discernment, the other in devotion" (*Canticle* [trans. S. J. Eales], xlix.4).

In several places in his writings, Bernard describes his own mystical, contemplative experiences of God. He included, for example, a beautiful piece of autobiography in his seventy-fourth sermon on the Song of Songs. "It was only by the movement of my heart that I was enabled to recognize His presence, and to know the might of His power by the sudden departure of vices and the strong restraint put upon all carnal affections." He went on to describe how he experienced the Word (Christ) as the Bridegroom of his soul, and how he perceived the loveliness of his beauty. "But when the Word withdrew Himself, all these spiritual powers and faculties began to droop and languish, as if the fire had been withdrawn from a bubbling pot."

Today we are hardly familiar with this kind of Christian language. Bernard's exposition of the Song of Songs takes the Lord Jesus Christ as the Bridegroom of the church, and the eternal Word, who was made flesh, as the Bridegroom of each Christian soul. Between the Lord and the church and every believer within the church is a love affair, a communion of spirits, a delighting and an affectionate embrace. "Let him kiss me with the kisses of his mouth" [1:1] signifies nothing else than to receive the inpouring of the Holy Spirit, by whose presence the divine love affair can proceed.

The contemplation of the heart that comes to those who wait upon the Bridegroom may occur in this manner:

> After a soul has been thus pressed by frequent aspirations towards God, or rather by continual prayer, and is afflicted by its longings, it is sometimes the case that He who is so earnestly desired and longed for, has pity on that soul and makes Himself manifest to it; and I think that, led by its own experience, it will be able to say with the prophet, "The Lord is good to them that wait for him, to the soul that seeketh Him" (*Canticle*, xxxi.4).

Or when head and heart are combined in faith, then contemplation may be described thus:

> When the Lord comes as a consuming fire and His Presence is understood in the power by which the soul is changed and in the love by which it is inflamed; when all stain of sin and rust of vices have been consumed in that fire, and the conscience has been purified and calmed, there ensues a certain, sudden and unwonted enlargement of mind and an inpouring of light illuminating the intellect, either for knowledge of Scripture or comprehension of mysteries. But not through open doors, but through narrow apertures does the ray of so great brightness penetrate, so long as this sorry wall of the body subsists (*Canticle*, lvii.7).

Only in the life of heaven will the redeemed find open doors rather than narrow openings for the entrance of the Light.

Though I am utterly taken with Bernard's exposition of the Song of Songs, I also am drawn often to his book *On the Love of God*. In this he draws a map of the development of love in the soul as it grows in the obedience of faith. From the attempts to love God for our own sake and the neighbor "as you love yourself," we move on to attempting to love God for what he has done, and continues to do for us, as our Savior. The third stage is loving God because of who he is (rather than for what he has done for us) and thus loving myself and my neighbor as God's creation. The final stage to which we ought to aspire is loving myself wholly for God's sake and loving my neighbor also wholly for God's sake. In words that recall the teaching of Augustine, Bernard wrote:

> Happy is he who hath deserved to reach unto the fourth degree of love, where man may love not even himself except for the sake of God. This love is a mountain, and the high mountain of God. When shall the mind experience affection like this, so that, inebriated with divine love, forgetful of self, and become to its own self like a broken vessel, it may utterly pass over into God, and, adhering to God, become one spirit with him? Blessed and holy should I call one to whom it has been granted to experience such a thing in this mortal life at rare intervals, or even once, and this suddenly, and for the space of hardly a moment. For in a certain manner to lose thyself, as though thou wert not, and to be utterly unconscious of thyself, and to be emptied of thyself, and, as it were, brought to nothing, pertains to celestial conversation, not to human condition. And if, indeed, any mortal is suddenly, now and then (as has been said), and for a moment, admitted to this, straightway the wicked world envies, the evil of the day disturbs, the body of death becomes a burden, the necessity of flesh provokes, the defect of corruption does not endure, and, what is more insistent than these, fraternal charity recalls. Alas! he is compelled to return unto himself, to fall back into his own, and miserably to exclaim: "Unhappy man that I am, who shall deliver me from the body of this death?" (*On the Love of God*, 27).

Happily these temporary glances into heaven and tastings of the love of God are open to all who practice the contemplation of the heart and to all whom God chooses to visit. The Bridegroom always has the final say.

CONCLUSION

Both Augustine and Bernard find a necessary connection between God's revealed truth, recorded in Holy Scripture, meditation or consideration upon that truth, and the mystical knowing or experiencing of Truth (God in Christ).

Both obviously and clearly teach a mysticism of love. Yet there are important differences between the two saints, and they illustrate that while God certainly calls us to know him, we do not all come to that vital knowledge in precisely the same ways.

Bernard opens a new chapter in the exposition of contemplation in the Western church. It draws its power from his appreciation and understanding of the affective depths of human nature. Only in the heart is man truly engaged, for deep feeling is greater than deep thought. In spirituality it is the Deep calling the deep, as it were, and thus God calls to the heart. Certainly knowledge is important, but knowledge alone is bad; thought and feeling, head and heart belong together. But we are primarily moved by our feelings, and thus feelings are deeper than thought. So Bernard teaches a contemplation of the heart where the intellect and knowledge are secondary though important. For him the ascent to God ends in rapture, a foretaste of heaven, the kiss of the Bridegroom.

In contrast, there appears to be no disjunction of thought and feeling for Augustine. For him knowledge and feeling so belong together that either without the other is inconceivable. Here he stands with Plato, who taught that the center of unity in man is his intelligence, and there feeling and thought are united. For Augustine the quest of the soul is to know God and knowing him to love him. The brief moment of rapture that occurs occasionally is a moment of understanding, of enlightenment, of "seeing" Truth, where feeling is within the understanding.

The separation of thought from feeling and of theology from spirituality, which began in the Middle Ages, has become a permanent factor in Western Christianity. To have a spirituality like that of Augustine where the head carries the heart has become extremely difficult for Christians in modern times. So often the choice seems to be either a contemplation of the mind or a contemplation of the heart.

CHAPTER 8

Meditation—John Owen and Richard Baxter

*I*n the 1680s and toward the end of his life, John Owen, the former Dean of Christ Church, Oxford, and at that time pastor of a small Congregational church in London, published several important books on the topic of meditation, contemplation, and spiritual mindedness. It may justly be claimed that prayerfully to consider and delight in the Lord Jesus Christ in the glory of heaven was regarded by many Anglicans and Puritans in the seventeenth century as the essential content of mental and contemplative prayer.

This emphasis was not intended to bypass or neglect the accounts of Jesus in Galilee and Judea as found in the Gospels. Rather it was to meditate upon the living, reigning Jesus as the Lord of lords and to see his incarnation, ministry, death, and resurrection from this perspective. Thus Jesus was not merely a historical figure but the One who is the same yesterday, today, and forever. Therefore, in considering the teaching or the miracles of Jesus the aim was to think of them as the words and deeds of the One who now sits at the right hand of the Father and whose saving work begun in space and time now continues outside space and time, both for those in heaven and for those on earth.

We can trace this approach back both to Augustine, who often wrote of heavenly meditation, and to John Calvin of Geneva, who, in his *Institutes of the Christian Religion* (Book III, chap. 9), sets out the basic duty of contemplating Christ in his heavenly glory. In England this meditative approach to the exalted Lord Jesus was given special emphasis by the first major book on meditation, *The Art of Divine Meditation* (1606) by Bishop Joseph Hall of Norwich.

Further, it was the central topic of the best-known book on meditation from English Puritans, *The Saints' Everlasting Rest* by Richard Baxter, to which we shall turn below.

We may claim that the general position of Owen and his fellow Puritans both in Old and New England was that the renewal of the mind by the mercies of God and through the Holy Spirit primarily occurs when the mind is occupied in considering and adoring God incarnate, the Lord Jesus Christ in his heavenly glory. And we may add that no writer presented this duty with more power and clarity than did John Owen. However, because he did not write in the popular mode (in contrast to Richard Baxter) and because his style is classicist, the depths and insights of his teaching were accessible only to the educated readers of his time.

Owen came to his spiritual ascent to God from within a clearly thought-out Reformed or Calvinist theology. He had a profound sense of the glorious sovereignty of God and often meditated upon this as well as upon the covenant of grace whose origin is in the eternal decrees of the Triune Lord. For Owen "the chief end of man is to glorify God and enjoy him forever." The purpose of biblical and theological knowledge, which is extremely important, is to lead the affections of the soul to love God and delight in God as the living God, the God of the covenant of grace. This loving and delighting is possible only when the Holy Spirit enlightens the whole soul and inspires and enables it to ascend to the heavenlies to contemplate Christ there.

SPIRITUAL MINDEDNESS

The title page of Owen's book on spiritual mindedness had these words: *Phronēma Tou Pneumatos: or, the Grace and Duty of Being Spiritually Minded, declared and improved* (1681). Then followed two Bible verses: "To be spiritually minded is life and peace" (Rom. 8:6, KJV) and "Set your affection on things above" (Col. 3:2, KJV).

In chapter seven Owen supplied a concise definition of spiritual mindedness:

> To be spiritually minded is, not to have the notion and knowledge of spiritual things in our minds; it is not to be constant, no, nor to abound, in the performance of duties: both which may be where there is no grace in the heart at all. It is to have our minds really exercised with delight about heavenly things, the things that are above, especially Christ himself as at the right hand of God.

Of course, Owen did not mean that the believer had no need for knowledge in the mind. In fact, he urged Christians to know the content—in fact to learn by heart—the content of Holy Scripture. Rather, he was insisting here that unless one had a genuine personal relationship with and delight in the Lord Jesus, knowledge is merely cerebral and doctrinal. The knowledge God looks for arises when the mind is in the heart and by it the affections (love, delight, reverence, etc.) are directed to heaven.

On the same page, explaining what are heavenly things, he wrote this of Jesus Christ, the Lord in heaven:

> I speak now with an especial respect unto him in heaven; the glory of his presence, as God and man eternally united; the discharge of his mediatory office, as he is at the right hand of God; the glory of his present acting of the church, as he is the minister of the sanctuary and the true tabernacle which God hath fixed

and not man; the love, power, and efficacy of his
intercession, whereby he takes care for the accomplish-
ment of the salvation of the church; the approach of his
glorious coming unto judgment,—are to be the objects
of our daily thoughts and meditations.

Such topics represent not only knowledge of actual scriptural
teaching but also a certain development of Christological
doctrine (as found in the Nicene Creed and repeated in the
Catechisms and Confessions of the Protestant Reformation).
However, in order to ascertain precisely the content of such
meditation we need only turn to and read his *Meditations
and Discourses on the Glory of Christ* (1684).

Applying Paul's teaching in Romans 8:6, Owen insisted
that "to be spiritually minded is the great distinguishing
character of true believers from all unregenerate persons"
and that "where anyone is spiritually minded, there, and
there alone, is life and peace." Within the duty of being
spiritually minded he saw three essential requirements:

1. The actual exercise of the mind, in its thoughts,
meditations, and desires, about things spiritual and
heavenly. So is it expressed in the verse foregoing [8:5]:
"They that are after the flesh do mind the things of the
flesh,"—they think on them, their contrivances are
about them, and their desires after them; "but they that
are after the Spirit do mind the things of the Spirit." They
mind them by fixing their thoughts and meditations
upon them.

2. The inclination, disposition, and frame of the mind, in
all its affections, whereby it adheres and cleaves unto
spiritual things. This "minding of the Spirit" resides
habitually in the affections. Wherefore, the phronēma of
the Spirit, or the mind as renewed and acted by a
spiritual principle of light and life, is the exercise of its
thoughts, meditations, and desires, on spiritual things,
proceeding from the love and delight of its affections in
them and engagement unto them.

3. A complacency of mind, from that gust, relish, and
savour, which it finds in spiritual things, from their
suitableness unto its constitution, inclinations, and

desires. There is a salt in spiritual things, whereby they are condited and made savoury unto a renewed mind; though to others they are as the white of an egg, that hath no taste or savour in it. In this gust and relish lies the sweetness and satisfaction of spiritual life. Speculative notions about spiritual things, when they are alone, are dry, sapless, and barren. In this gust we taste by experience that God is gracious, and that the love of Christ is better than wine, or whatever else hath the most grateful relish unto a sensual appetite. This is the proper foundation of that "joy which is unspeakable and full of glory."

We rarely use complacency today with the intended sense of Owen. We would say pleasure or satisfaction of mind. Owen wrote, "This holy complacency, this rest and sweet repose of mind, is the foundation of the delight of believers in this duty. They do not pray only because it is their duty so to do, nor yet because they stand in need of it, so as that they cannot live without it, but they have delight in it; and to keep them from it is all one has to keep them from their daily food and refreshment."

MEDITATING

Owen distinguished unstructured and semi-spontaneous meditation from "solemn and stated meditation." Of the latter he wrote:

By solemn or stated meditation, I intend the thoughts of some subject spiritual and divine, with the fixing, forcing, and ordering of our thoughts about it, with a design to affect our own hearts and souls with the matter of it, of the things contained in it. By this design it is distinguished from the study of the word, wherein our principal aim is to learn the truth, or to declare it unto others; and so also from prayer, whereof God himself is the immediate object. But in meditation it is the affecting of our own hearts and minds with love, delight, and humiliation.

Owen was too much a pastor not to recognize that some Christians were not only unskillful in but also unable to perform stated meditation. Yet their souls were often filled with spiritual thoughts of God and the Lord Jesus Christ. They were able and desirous to think of and delight in their heavenly Savior and to be filled with gratitude and joy because of his love for them. Therefore Owen encouraged believers often to consider and have joy in their Lord above according to their full potential and God-given ability. This meant frequent, occasional meditation for all, with the added duty of solemn meditation for those able to engage in it (such as pastors and lay leaders).

A particular emphasis of Owen is upon the crucial place of faith in meditation and contemplation. Consideration and reflection proceed from the believing heart, which is consciously setting aside sin and worldliness. Genuine faith exists only in a repentant heart where sin is being mortified. Thus where faith exists in the soul, with it is an in-built divine movement toward love and faithfulness. However, faith can so easily be choked and perverted where there is not constant watchfulness and spiritual discipline. As Owen remarked, "Where corrupt lusts or inordinate affections are indulged unto, where they are not continually mortified, where any one sin hath a perplexing prevalency in the mind, faith will be so far weakened thereby, as that it can neither see nor meditate upon this glory of Christ in due manner."

Concerning the heavenly glory of Christ, Owen explained that we must consider two aspects—its particular nature and its necessary effect. He wrote:

> The first is, a spiritual perception or understanding of it as revealed in the Scriptures. For the revelation of the glory of his person, office, and grace, is the principal subject of them, and the principal object of our faith. And the other consists in multiplied thoughts about him, with actings of faith, in love, trust, delight, and longing after the full enjoyment of him, 1 Peter i.8. If we satisfy ourselves in mere notions and speculations about

the glory of Christ as doctrinally revealed unto us, we shall find no transforming power or efficacy communicated unto us thereby. But when, under the conduct of that spiritual light, our affections do cleave unto him with full purpose of heart, our minds are filled with the thoughts of him and delight in him, and faith is kept up unto its constant exercise in trust and affiance on him,—virtue will proceed from him to purify our hearts, increase our holiness, strengthen our graces, and to fill us sometimes "with joy unspeakable and full of glory." This is the just temperature of a state of spiritual health,—namely, when our light of the knowledge of the glory of God in Christ doth answer the means of it which we enjoy, and when our affections unto Christ do hold proportion unto that light; and this according unto the various degrees of it,—for some have more, and some have less. Where light leaves the affections behind, it ends in formality or atheism; and where affections outrun light they sink in the bog of superstition, doting on images and pictures, or the like. But where things go not into these excesses, it is better that our affections exceed our light from the defect of our understanding, than that our light exceed our affections from the corruption of our wills. In both these is the exercise of faith frequently interrupted and obstructed by the remainder of corruption in us, especially if not kept constantly under discipline of mortification, but some way indulged unto.

Anyone who carefully considers these words and who has some experience of the life of prayer will recognize great wisdom in what he writes of the relationship of thoughts about God and joy in God.

THE GODLY AFFECTIONS

"The great contest of heaven and earth is about the affections of the poor worm which we call man," wrote Owen. In infinite condescension and grace God expressly says, "My son, give me your heart" (Prov. 23:26). In the Mosaic administration of the covenant of grace the Lord God required his people, Israel, "to fear the LORD your God, to walk in all his ways, to love him, to serve the LORD your God with all your heart and with all your soul" (Deut. 10:12). And to this end "the LORD your God will circumcise your hearts . . . so that you may love him with all your heart and with all your soul" (Deut. 30:6).

Owen was convinced that by our affections we can give away what we are and what we have. Thus he wrote:

> Affections are in the soul as the helm in the ship; if it be laid hold on by a skilful hand, he turneth the whole vessel which way he pleaseth. If God hath the powerful hand of his grace upon our affections, he turns our souls unto a compliance with his institutions, instructions, in mercy, afflictions, trials, all sorts of providences, and holds them firm against all winds and storms of temptation, that they shall not hurry them on pernicious dangers. Such a soul alone is tractable and pliable unto all intimations of God's will.

However, if the skillful hand is the world or the devil via aspects of culture, philosophy, or worldiness, then the affections are earthly, not heavenly, and fleshly, not spiritual. For, as the apostle John declared, "If anyone loves the world, the love of the Father is not in him" (1 John 2:15).

Following the apostle Paul, Augustine, and the Reformed tradition, Owen taught that "nothing in the nature of man, no power or faculty of the soul, is fallen under greater disorder and depravation by the entrance of sin than the affections." He pointed out that the ancient philosophers of Greece and Rome recognized only weakness in the rational mind but disorder and tumult in the affections so as to render the soul "like a troubled sea, whose waters cast up mire and dirt." And he quoted the words of Jesus, "Out of the heart come evil thoughts, murder, adultery, sexual immorality, theft, false testimony, slander" (Matt. 15:19). Therefore, because of indwelling sin, human affections constitute what Owen described as "an utter aversation [turning away] from God and all spiritual things" and "an inordinate cleaving unto things vain, earthly and sensual, causing the soul to engage into the pursuit of them as the horse rushes into battle."

Since the powerful effect of sin upon the soul is to bring spiritual death, what each person needs is a new principle of life in the soul from God himself. The Gospel of God concerning Jesus Christ promises just this, and the Holy Spirit himself provides it by his own presence as indwelling Spirit. "When our affections are inclined by the saving grace of the Holy Spirit, then they are renewed . . . no other change will give them a spiritual renovation." Thus the fruit of the Spirit as described by Paul in Galatians 5:22–23 represents the natural affections of the soul renovated and renewed by grace. "Love, joy, peace, patience, kindness, goodness, faith-fulness, gentleness and self-control" are the affections, and "they continue the same as they were in their essence, substance, and natural powers; but are changed in their properties, qualities, inclinations, whenever a new nature is given unto them" by the Holy Spirit, who works the cure by "the love of God, proceeding from faith in him by Christ Jesus."

Like the great American theologian Jonathan Edwards, who also studied the affections (see his masterly *The Religious Affections*), Owen carefully distinguished the merely transient, temporary, and occasional impressions made upon the affections from the all-embracing effect caused by the renovation of grace through spiritual regeneration and sanc-tification. For example "there may be a [temporary or superficial] change in the affections, wherein men may have delight in the duties of religious worship and diligence in their observance; but it is the spiritual renovation of the affections that gives delight in God through Christ, in any duty of religious worship whatever."

For the regenerate and being-sanctified believer, the delight in worship is not in the externals as such but in the living God, the Father, the Son, and the Holy Spirit, via the externals. To put it a different way, believers make use of the streams but only as a means of communication with the spring. The various aspects and parts of Christian worship, fellowship, and devotion "are appointed by God as a blessed means of communion and intercourse between himself in Christ and their souls." For by them Christ "doth communicate his love and grace unto us and in and by them do we act faith and love on him." To summarize: "Our souls have no way of approach unto God in duties of worship but by faith; no way of adherence or cleaving unto him but by love; no way of abiding in him but by fear, reverence, and delight."

In this paradox of grace and in this covenantal relationship, it is God who effectually calls his children into a vital, personal relationship with himself; and he does so through his Word and Spirit. As the mind is in the heart or as the whole soul trusts in, looks unto, and delights in God, then the believer knows experientially what is genuine, personal communion with God the Father through God the Son by God the Holy Spirit. Owen wrote about this communion with God not merely on the basis of scriptural teaching but also from his own firsthand experience of fellowship with God in the depths of prayer, meditation, and contemplation, both in corporate worship and personal devotion.

In order to delight in God with great joy, Owen insisted that the affections had to be wholly under the leading and direction of faith. "We can love nothing sincerely with divine love but what we believe savingly with divine faith." In believing the divine promises as given in Holy Scripture and trusting in God on their basis, the regenerate soul will see by faith and thereby present unto the affections spiritual and heavenly things in their true nature, beauty, and excellency as God wishes them to be known by his covenant people now. "The end God designs is, to draw our hearts and affections unto himself: and unto this end, he gives unto us a glorious internal light, whereby we may be enabled to discern the true nature of the things that we are to cleave unto with love and delight." Thus by and in faith we are so to meditate upon and contemplate spiritual and heavenly things (the Lord Jesus, King, Priest, and Prophet in heaven) so that our affections are more and more renewed and in themselves made more spiritual and heavenly.

Owen went to great lengths to explain that delighting in God through faith and by contemplative prayer must not be confused with a merely imaginative meditation. He was very conscious of the power of human imagination to create a seemingly real world, which in essence is only make-belief. So he explained that meditating and contemplating in and by faith involves beginning from and going no further than God's revealed promises and descriptions in Holy Scripture allow. It was in this area that he made his few criticisms of certain Roman Catholic devotions, accusing them of creating super-stition rather than true devotion, for the object set before the affections was not the true Christ of Scripture but that of images, icons, and pictures. For Owen there is true devotion only when the affections are delighting in the Christ of Scripture. And only in such delighting is there a genuine moving of the soul toward perfection ("not that we can attain perfection by it, but that therein our souls are in progress toward perfection").

FAITH AND SIGHT CONTRASTED

Owen often explained that the view we have here on earth by faith of the glory of Christ is gathered by us from different places within Holy Scripture. "It is the wisdom of faith to gather into one those parcelled descriptions that are given of him [in various places in the Bible] that they may be the object of its view and contemplation." In contrast, "in the vision we shall have above, the whole glory of Christ will be at once and always represented unto us: and we shall be enabled in one act of the light of glory to comprehend it." Again, here in our earthly pilgrimage of faith, we are often at a loss, for "our minds and understandings fail us in their contemplations." But in the glory of heaven all the faculties of the soul will without any weakness or hindrance exercise their perfect operations on the most perfect object (God in Christ). And thereby the full blessedness of which human nature is capable will be experienced by the perfected soul. We must allow Owen to explain this matter in his own way:

> In the vision which we shall have above, the whole glory of Christ will be at once and always represented unto us; and we shall be enabled in one act of the light of glory to comprehend it. Here, indeed, we are at a loss;—our minds and understandings fail us in their contemplations. It will not yet enter into our hearts to conceive what is the beauty, what is the glory of this complete representation of Christ unto us. To have at once all the glory of what he is, what he was in his outward state and condition, what he did and suffered, what he is exalted unto,—his love and condescension, his mystical union with the church, and the communication of himself unto it, with the recapitulation of all things in him,—and the glory of God, even the Father, in his wisdom, righteousness, grace, love, goodness, power, shining forth eternally in him, in what he is, hath done, and doth,—all presented unto us in one view, all comprehended by us at once, is that which at present we cannot conceive. We can long for it, pant after it, and have some foretastes of it,—namely, of that state and season wherein our whole souls, in all their powers and faculties, shall constantly, inseparably, eternally cleave by love unto the whole Christ, in the sight of the glory of his person and grace, until they are watered, dissolved, and inebriated in the waters of life and the rivers of pleasure that are above for evermore. So must we speak of the things which we admire, which we adore, which we love, which we long for, which we have some foretastes of in sweetness ineffable, which yet we cannot comprehend.

Such are some of the differences between faith and sight.

For Owen the delighting by faith in the living God through Jesus Christ is the inner quality of the Christian life, and as such is the source of the movement toward maturity in faith, hope, and love. Heavenly mindedness or spiritual mindedness is therefore not only the specific mindset into which God calls his covenant children, but it is also the indispensable source of the life of practical service of God and neighbor. Meditating and contemplating (Owen seems to use these words interchangeably) by faith the glory of Christ above cannot be separated from a real, biblical understanding of the Christian life. There can be no transformation and renewal without such mental prayer.

RICHARD BAXTER

In the very readable *The Saints' Everlasting Rest* (1649; 9th ed., 1662), Baxter carefully expounded Hebrews 4:9, "There remains . . . a Sabbath-rest for the people of God." He urged his readers to accept the call to sanctification and holiness, a maturing in faith, hope, and love, with the utmost seriousness and with deep commitment. To forward this goal of perfection for Jesus' sake, Baxter pressed upon each of his readers "the set and solemn acting of all the powers of the soul in meditation upon thy everlasting rest," the Sabbath rest of the kingdom of God in heaven, where God is all in all. Such fixed and serious meditation is in contrast to what he called "transient" or occasional meditation when "in the midst of business we have some good thoughts of God in our minds."

To meditate upon the Sabbath rest is "a walk to Mount Zion; from the kingdoms of this world to the kingdom of saints; from time to eternity; it is walking upon sun, moon and stars, in the garden and paradise of God." Before the walk can begin there must be preparation of mind and heart: or as Baxter put it, there is a "setting of thy heart in tune" before the music of meditation and contemplation can begin and before the affections can be moved to delight in God.

Baxter has no doubt but that the mental activity of

consideration "is the great instrument by which this heavenly work is done." For it is only in the act of considering God's truth that the door between the head and heart is opened. "The understanding having received truths lays them up in the memory and consideration conveys them from thence to the affections." Further, "consideration presents to the affections those things which are most important." For we all know that "the most delightful object does not entertain, where it is not seen, nor the most joyful news affect him that does not hear it." In fact consideration "presents the most important things in the most affecting way." It exalts reason to its just authority by placing it upon the throne of the soul. If reason is not in this highest place, then the senses dominate and the soul is confused and misled. Thus "consideration exalts the object of faith and comparatively disgraces the objects of sense." And it "makes reason strong and active" to serve the cause of heavenly contemplation.

Here is how Baxter described the act of meditation upon the everlasting rest of the people of God:

> It is by consideration that we first have recourse to the memory and from thence take those heavenly doctrines which we intend to make the subject of our meditation—such as promises of eternal life, descriptions of the saints' glory, the resurrection &c. We then present them to our judgment that it may deliberately view them over and take an exact survey and determine uprightly concerning the perfection of our celestial happiness, against all the dictates of flesh and sense, and so as to magnify the Lord in our hearts till we are filled with a holy admiration—But the principal thing is to exercise, not merely our judgment, but our faith in the truth of the everlasting rest; by which I mean both the truth of the promises and of our own personal interest in them. If we did really and firmly believe that there is such a glory and that within a few days our eyes shall behold it, O what passions would it raise within us! What love, what longing would it excite within us. O how it would actuate every affection! . . . Never expect to have love and joy move, when faith stands still, which must lead the

way. Therefore, daily exercise faith, and set before it the freeness of the promise, God's urging all to accept it, Christ's gracious disposition, all the evidences of the love of Christ, his faithfulness to his engagements and the evidences of his love in ourselves; lay all these together, and think, whether they do not testify the good-will of the Lord concerning our salvation, and may not properly be pleaded against our unbelief. Thus when the judgment hath determined, and faith hath apprehended the truth of our happiness, then may our meditation proceed to raise our affections and, particularly, love, desire, hope, courage or boldness and joy.

So in the act of meditation the affections—love, desire, hope, boldness, and joy—are stirred up either singly or together through the consideration by faith of God's promises. As the affections are raised, so the believer knows the sweet and the holy experience of the presence of the Lord. For to those who rise by faith the Lord descends in grace in a holy encounter. And the result of such meditation is the strengthening of the grace of God in the soul and the determination to live wholly for Christ in the world of sin.

Meditation or contemplation are for Owen and Baxter necessarily personal duties and experiences. However, both also tied them to the weekly meeting of the Lord's people for worship. They encouraged meditation/contemplation before the service to prepare for it, meditation during the service (and especially at the Lord's Table and in hearing the Lord's Word preached) to benefit from it, and then after the service to appropriate the fruit of divine worship. We must also note that they are nearer to Bernard than to Augustine in that for them knowledge leads to the warming of the affections, and then the mind sees, loves, delights, and rejoices through the heart. So it is not surprising that Jonathan Edwards in his *The Religious Affections* taught with great clarity that true religion is in the affections—even though he truly contemplated the glory of God in heaven and on earth.

CHAPTER 9

Contemplation—
Teresa of Avila and
John of the Cross

*I*n seeking to understand the Catholic doctrine of mysticism or contemplative prayer, we could make use of post-Reformation writers such as Pierre de Berulle, Jean-Pierre de Caussade, and Jean Nicolas Grou, all of whom wrote attractively on prayer and mysticism. I have chosen, however, to present the teaching of Teresa of Avila (1515–1582), the Spanish Carmelite nun, a woman of great practical ability, strong character, and shrewdness. She was the first writer to describe psychologically the states of prayer that come between the practice of basic mental prayer or discursive meditation and the vital spiritual union (the mystical marriage) of the soul with God in contemplation.

Her life, work, and writings prove that to be heavenly minded does not make a person to be practically useless on earth. In fact she was a beautiful woman with curly chestnut hair and a magnetic personality. However, her "conversion" of 1555, described in the ninth chapter of her autobiography, heralded the beginings of her ever-growing series of mystical, contemplative experiences that enlarged her soul and ennobled her character. She was fifty-two when she began her major foundations of convents in Spain and, according to contemporaries, she was as attractive, eloquent, and lively as ever, and endowed with an irresistible charm.

In 1970 she was declared to be a "Doctor of the Church" because of the theological content of her writings on prayer. This honor granted to her should indicate to us that she was a serious writer and intended her work for those both inside and outside the cloister who truly wanted to know, love, and serve God. Because she uses ordinary yet attractive images, she has been taken by many as teaching that the life of prayer is basically easy and only a matter of the right method or technique. This is a major misunderstanding of her intentions. In fact, her simple style points to depth, not shallowness. She usually wrote down her thoughts and described her experiences of communion with God because her spiritual director asked her to do so in order to help and encourage others in the path of virtue and prayer.

Teresa of Avila wrote several major works including *The Way of Perfection*, *Life* (her autobiography), *Foundations*, and *The Interior Castle*. The last is not only her most mature work; it is also a genuine spiritual classic in which she describes the development of prayer from its beginnings to its maturation as a means of intimate, joyous adoration of and union with God himself through Jesus Christ.

ILLUSTRATIVE IMAGES

In *The Interior Castle* Teresa used a variety of images to illustrate the experience of our relationship with God in its various stages. The two most important are the use of water in irrigation and the medieval Spanish castle.

To appreciate the first we have to place ourselves in Spain in the sixteenth century and recall how a garden, field, or vineyard was watered. Several methods were available to bring physical water to the places where it was needed. There was the hard work of lifting water from a well in a bucket and then pouring it on the garden. A second way, requiring less exertion, involved the use of a waterwheel and the channeling of water to run through a viaduct to the places of need. The third, requiring even less effort, was to make use of a nearby stream or river, diverting the water as needed to flow into the garden. The fourth and best way, which required no effort at all, was the gift of gentle and abundant rainfall from the heavens sent by the Lord himself.

If we think of our souls as gardens needing water, this illustration helps us to see that while prayer begins with our working hard at concentration and content, it can and ought to mature into such a relationship with God that he graciously and gently initiates and sustains it.

To appreciate the second we need first of all to picture a Spanish castle with its moat, drawbridge, high stone walls, and many rooms inside. Then, second, we need to picture a single diamond or a pure crystal through which light is perfectly reflected. Having these pictures in our imagination, we then need to listen carefully to Teresa to appreciate her development of them when she says that the soul is as it were "a castle made of a single diamond or of a very clear crystal, in which are many rooms. Just as in heaven there are many mansions." In the very center is the pure light, the sun, and the path of prayer is to go through the rooms into the perfect light. Christians are to be as capable of knowing and enjoying God as the crystal is in reflecting the light.

This is how Teresa explained the relationships of the sets of rooms or mansions to the very center of the castle, which is the king's own unique room:

> You must not imagine these mansions as arranged in a row, one behind another, but fix your attention on the centre, the room or palace occupied by the King. Think of a palmito, which has many outer rinds surrounding the savoury part within, all of which must be taken away before the center can be eaten. Just so around this central room are many more, as there also are above it. In speaking of the soul we must always think of it as

spacious, ample and lofty: and this can be done without the least exaggeration, for the soul's capacity is much greater than we can realize, and this Sun which is in the palace, reaches every part of it.

Teresa assumes not only that the living God indwells the soul of every true Christian, but that as the Light he desires to cause his light to flood the whole of the soul—mind, heart, and will. Prayer is the divinely provided means whereby the indwelling Light of lights not only illuminates but also purifies and ennobles the soul. In doing so he prepares it for fullness of light and life in an immortalized and glorified body in the heavenly Jerusalem (Rev. 21).

In her *Interior Castle* Teresa explains the seven mansions or sets of rooms through which the believing, prayerful soul passes in its journey in faith and love toward God who is both transcendent (she calls him "His Majesty" often) and immanent (indwelling the soul). The movement from one set of rooms to the next is, however, not so simple as if it were a physical journey through a medieval castle. In the life of prayer actual progression toward God is not only gradual but is also recognized only after it has occurred. Further, as Teresa explained, "there is no closed door to separate the one from the other," and so one may experience regression as well as progression.

In what follows I shall explain the journey through the seven mansions and also point out the parallel interpretation of this journey through the image of water for the garden of the soul. The pilgrimage is told from the viewpoint of the one who travels in, with, and through Jesus Christ to God the Father by the power of the Holy Spirit. Therefore, while it is hands-on biblical doctrine, it is a psychological, not a doctrinal, analysis and description.

However, first of all, it is absolutely necessary to make clear that Teresa insisted that the path of prayer is also the path of holiness and sanctification. The bringing of the sinful human will into conformity with the divine will (as Rom.

12:1–2 insists) is of primary importance and, in comparison with this necessity, any cultivation of methods or techniques of meditation and prayer are secondary. One of her choice remarks is that "this King does not give himself but to those who give themselves entirely to him." Therefore, while a person might be successful in using methods of meditation and mental prayer, the higher levels of communion with God are inaccessible except to the believer who dedicates himself to the will of God.

So it is not surprising that she insists on the constant need for personal purification in the rooting out from our lives that which we know is not pleasing to our Lord. She taught that God will not lead his children into the inner mansions until they are both ready and desirous of the experience in store for them there. The zealous practice of Christian virtue is the context in which a life of true prayer ought to be set. She described humility "as the principal virtue which must be practiced by those who pray."

Further, Teresa was conscious of human weakness, and she emphasized over and over again the need for determination and perseverance. She wrote:

> It is most important—all important indeed—that they should begin well by making an earnest and most determined resolve not to halt until they reach their goal, whatever may come, whatever may happen to them, however hard they may have to labor, whoever may complain of them, whether they reach their goal or die on the road or have no heart to confront the trials which they meet, whether the very world dissolves before them.

The fainthearted are not likely to mature in prayer. "Because you are lukewarm—neither hot nor cold—I am about to spit you out of my mouth" (Rev. 3:16), says our Lord. For Teresa it is always true that we are to love him because he first loved us and continues to love us everlastingly with a perfect love, despite our unworthiness.

THE PATH OF PRAYER—THE BEGINNINGS

The first three sets of mansions represent the beginnings of the devout life and the entering into a serious, prayerful, relationship with God through faith in Christ. This means both the desire to confess and depart from all known sin and the giving up of all attachments and activities that have the effect of discouraging or opposing the path of true spirituality. Only in this manner does the nominal become the committed Christian.

Teresa urged believers not only to join wholeheartedly in vocal prayer in church and at home but also to make the space and time to engage in mental prayer or meditation. By this means she believed that hearts can be warmed and the will directed toward God in genuine prayer. Interestingly, she had little to say about methods of mental prayer; in fact she believed that too much discursive thinking in meditation could hinder the opening of the soul unto the living God. "If you would progress a long way on this road and ascend to the mansions of your desire, the important thing is not to think much, but to love much," she wrote.

Specifically, the first set of rooms or mansions points to the basics, the very beginnings of the way of holiness. For "the light which comes from the central palace occupied by the King hardly reaches these first mansions at all: for, although they are not dark and black, as when the soul is in a state of sin, they are to some extent darkened." In these rooms are snakes and vipers that have entered with the soul and want to poison it so that it cannot desire or see the Light. Thus at this stage the soul is so absorbed in things of this world and so immersed in personal goals and business that it can hardly see yet the beauty and glory of the Lord. Here prayer is hard work and comes only with much effort. Perseverance and commitment are necessary.

The second set of mansions is the stage where the soul is beginning to hear God and be conscious of his presence—

not all the time but sometimes. These rooms are also the place where Satan realizes that he has a fight on his hands and begins to try to recapture the soul that is slipping away from his grasp. Further, at this stage the Christian virtues are "young"; they "have not yet learned to walk—in fact, they have only just been born." So there is a kind of tug-of-war going on, with the Lord pulling from one direction (but unwilling to pull so hard as to violate the freedom of the soul) and the old, sinful human nature still clinging to the world, flesh, and devil. Prayer continues to be hard work and there is still need for perseverance and total dedication.

In the third set of mansions the soul has matured sufficiently to have begun "to fear the Lord" with a filial fear. The believer is seeking to walk humbly with God, Creator, Redeemer, Judge, and Bridegroom of his or her soul. The progression from the second to the third and movement in the third set of mansions are often the positive result of the experience of suffering. This is especially so when suffering is accepted as being not for righteousness' sake but because of the many imperfections of the soul. Too often, said Teresa, "we are fonder of spiritual sweetness than of crosses. Test us, O Lord, thou who knowest all truth, that we may know ourselves." Thus, even though progress is being made, the soul in these mansions is still "laboring under the burden of our miserable nature which is like a great load of earth" upon our backs. Prayer remains essentially possible only with determined effort and commitment. God himself has not yet intervened to make prayer into a genuine relationship.

In terms of the water image, the way of prayer in the first three mansions is like the activity of drawing up water in a bucket from a well and then carrying the water to where it is needed in the garden. Prayer is actively produced through reading or meditation and is always from the human soul toward God, looking for a response from God. It is not yet the experience of a movement of God into the soul to create fellowship and spiritual union.

To describe prayer in this way is not of course to deny that God is active through the invisible presence and work of the Holy Spirit seeking to cause human souls to desire holiness and love. Rather it is to speak of the state of the human soul in terms of its journey in prayer and its experience of grace and mercy. Only as there is deeper commitment with greater fervency of devotion and love for God will the Holy Spirit lead the soul into the more profound experience of contemplative prayer.

FOURTH MANSIONS

It is important to recognize that some seventy percent of the text of the book is used by Teresa to explain the last four sets of mansions. These describe the ever more intense height and depth of contemplative, infused prayer.

The initial step from the third to the fourth set of mansions will often occur, she says, without the one who is praying realizing it has happened. Human effort diminishes as God's initiative comes into operation in the soul. In terms of the water image, the human effort of drawing and transporting water is replaced by means that involve less and less human energy—the use of a waterwheel rather than a bucket into a well. Obviously this change is due to the presence of the Holy Spirit, who is progressively taking control of first the human will and then, later, of the intellect and imagination.

Specifically, the fourth mansions normally contain two aspects of infused prayer—recollection (being called by God to be aware that he is there) and the prayer of quiet. First of all, there is usually a sense and vital awareness of God's presence both in the soul and in the place where prayer is being offered. It is in this recollected state when the will is captivated by God that the prayer of quiet occurs:

> The soul is so satisfied with God that as long as the recollection lasts, the quiet and calm are not lost since

the will is united with God even though the two faculties are distracted; in fact, little by little the will brings the intellect and the memory back to recollection. Even though the will may not be totally absorbed, it is so well occupied, without knowing how, that no matter what efforts the other two faculties make, they cannot take away its contentment and joy.

At this stage the soul knows distractions, but the believer is united in will with the Lord and, held in this union, he knows and delights in God's presence.

Teresa insists that this prayer of quiet union with the Lord is always the gift of grace and cannot be brought into being by mere human will and intention. As she remarks:

This prayer, then, is a little spark of the Lord's true love which He begins to enkindle in the soul; and He desires that the soul grow in the understanding of what this love accompanied by delight is. For anyone who has experience, it is impossible not to understand soon that this little spark cannot be acquired. Yet, this nature of ours is so eager for delights that it tries everything; but it is quickly left cold because however much it may desire to light the fire and obtain this delight, it doesn't seem to be doing anything else than throwing water on it and killing it.

Therefore, the believer must be receptive, humble and loving.

Further, infused prayer is not and cannot be divorced from life. This form of communion with God creates deeper faith in the Lord Jesus, inspires readiness to do the will of God, causes growth of the fruit of the Spirit, and increases desire for a closer walk with God and knowledge of him.

FIFTH MANSIONS

This experience is an intensification of the prayer of quiet. Here not only the will but also the intellect and imagination are held in union with God, silenced by love and awe. From her experience Teresa writes:

The consolation, the sweetness, and the delight are incomparably greater than that experienced in the previous prayer . . . This prayer is a glorious foolishness, a heavenly madness . . . Often I had been as though bewildered and inebriated in this love . . . The soul would desire to cry out praises, and it is beside itself . . . it cannot bear so much joy . . . it would want to be all tongues so as to praise the Lord.

It may be said that at this stage in the journey to maturity of faith the soul knows the truth of Paul's claim that the love of God has been poured into it by the presence of the Holy Spirit (Rom. 5:5). Emerging from this prayer of union with the Lord the believer has an even more intense desire to praise God continually and to be wholly free from the guilt and power of sin.

In terms of the water image, the believer is now drawing water directly from a stream or river with minimum human effort.

SIXTH MANSIONS

In this remarkable castle the soul is now getting near to the rooms where the King dwells and where the pure Light shines. These rooms represent a further intensification of union with God in Jesus Christ—so much so that the soul is no longer conscious of the external world when engaged in prayer. Here there is spiritual ecstasy, rapture, and even bodily levitation—states that are within infused contemplation and thus not to be confused with any similar states brought on by drugs or sexual excitement.

Of bodily levitation Teresa writes:

When one sees one's body so elevated from the ground that even though the spirit carries it along after itself, and does so very gently if one does not resist, one's feelings are not lost. At least I was conscious in such a way that I could understand I was being elevated. There is revealed a majesty about the One who can do this that makes a person's hair stand on end, and there remains a strong fear of offending so awesome a God. Yet such fear is accompanied by a very great love for Him.

This fear is of course filial fear—the reverence and fear of God arising from the heart of a child of God in whose soul is the love of God.

Teresa also speaks of the spiritual experience of wounding. "It seems as though an arrow is thrust into the heart or into the soul itself." This is the wound of love, whose only cure is found beyond death in the beatific vision of God in the life of the age to come.

The union is certainly a union of love, and so at this stage it may also be called betrothal in preparation for spiritual marriage (in the seventh mansions). The believer at this stage is so much in love with the Lord Jesus that he or she ardently desires to be with him, to reflect his glory, and to promote his kingdom of love.

SEVENTH MANSIONS

This is the experience of transforming union and of spiritual marriage. It is open-ended in that this infused contemplation is of such a quality that while it has a beginning, it has no ending in this life. In fact it continues from glory to glory in the life of the world to come. The entry into these mansions is through an intellectual vision of the one holy and blessed Trinity. This is how Teresa describes the experience:

> First of all the spirit becomes enkindled and is illumined, as it were, by a cloud of the greatest brightness. It sees these three Persons, individually, and yet, by a wonderful kind of knowledge which is given to it, the soul realizes that most certainly and truly all these three Persons are one Substance and one Power and one Knowledge and one God alone; so that what we hold by faith the soul may be said here to grasp by sight, although nothing is seen by the eyes, either of the body or of the soul, for it is no ordinary vision.

The delight arising from this vision is so perfect that no words can describe it. This is because a full union, a union of Spirit with spirit, of God with his own image in a human being, is occurring. The believer knows that he or she is truly in Christ. The soul is filled with Light—"Christ in you, the hope of glory" (Col. 1:27).

In terms of the water image, the believer is now conscious of direct, gracious, spiritual refreshment from heaven, for it is as if the rain is falling gently and consistently upon the garden.

This spiritual marriage of the believer with Christ does not mean that absolute perfection has been reached. While the soul knows that Christ is her Bridegroom and that he lavishes love upon his bride, the believer has only reached a relative perfection, a maturity in faith, hope, and love; and in this state the believer is not exempted from the trials of life. In fact they come in full force, but in the soul is that peace, joy, and tranquillity that is beyond understanding; for the Spirit witnesses to the human spirit, enabling the believer truly to know that he or she is a child of God.

REFLECTION

Is the experience of the seventh mansions for the few or for all Christians? In her answer Teresa is very clear. The call of the Lord Jesus to be perfect on earth as the heavenly Father is perfect in heaven is a call to all disciples of the kingdom, to all the baptized. God wills and invites all his covenant partners to love him with all their heart, soul, mind, and strength. Therefore those who dedicate themselves wholly to God find that the Father consecrates them in Christ Jesus unto himself and his service. In this renewal of mind they are transformed so as to take less and less pleasure in earthly matters and more and more delight in God and his will.

The division between those who press on to perfection

in the knowing of God in the later mansions and those who merely maintain a status quo position in one of the early mansions is not a division between monks/nuns and laity. It is a division that cuts through the cloister as well as through the congregation of Christ's flock. Those who in and by grace reach the seventh mansion are not necessarily those who pray more; rather, they are those who believe and love more, who truly delight in God and contemplate the glory of God in the face of Jesus Christ.

JOHN OF THE CROSS

Experts point out that there are some differences between the teaching of Teresa and that of her friend, John of the Cross, on the movement of the soul from meditation and/or acquired contemplation, where the believer is the primary mover in search of God, to infused contemplation, where God initiates the contemplative prayer. This is probably what we should expect, for just where and when the one ends and the other begins is not absolutely clear. Each person who prays and seeks God is different, and the Lord speaks to people as persons, not robots.

However, it is clear that both Teresa and John of the Cross belong to a period that follows a time (the late medieval period) when there had been an intensive analysis of the theological virtues of faith, hope, and love. In this analysis faith was seen as the seed of eternal life, hope the mainstay of spiritual progress, and love as eternal life begun in the soul. Faith and not the keen intellect was understood as the basis of mystical contemplation, and calm love rather than struggle and effort as the right disposition of soul. So we find John of the Cross writing of the loving, receptive attention required for contemplative mysticism:

> When . . . the soul is conscious of being led into silence, and hearkens, it must forget even that practice of loving attention, so that it may remain free for that which the

> Lord desires of it . . . so that through contemplation it may receive that which is communicated to it from God. For we have already said that pure contemplation consists in receiving (*The Living Flame of Love*, iii, 35–36).

Similar sentiments are found in abundance in the writings of Teresa. Related to this receptivity is the doctrine of the supernatural infusion of knowledge and love by the Holy Spirit as the will of the believer is gradually bent by grace into the service of the Lord in daily obedience and the practice of the Christian virtues.

THE DARK NIGHT OF THE SOUL

Fray John (John of the Cross) met Madre Teresa of Jesus (Teresa of Avila) at Medina del Campo in Spain soon after his ordination in 1567. He was twenty-five and she was fifty-two, but their difference in age did not affect their esteem for and confidence in each other as fellow servants of the Lord Jesus in the new Carmelite Order. Teresa had every confidence in him as a spiritual director and she knew he was a holy man. Since he was only five feet tall, she would affectionately call him "the holy little Fray John" and "little Seneca."

Fray John, like Madre Teresa, wrote books to guide people in the path of holiness and contemplative prayer. John was a poet and has left a fine heritage of spiritual poetry. His book, *The Dark Night*, begins with a poem and is composed of an exposition of the poem. The first line is "One dark night." In this dark night God implements two purgations. John explained, "Souls begin to enter this dark night when God, gradually drawing out the state of beginners (those who practice meditation on the spiritual road), starts to place them in the state of proficients (those who are already contemplatives) so that by passing through this state they might reach that of the perfect, which is the divine union of the soul with God." To appreciate John's seemingly low estimate of meditation, it is important to realize that the rules for meditation in the monastic establishments at that time tended to make it very much a cerebral exercise of the discursive reason. It was primarily an exercise of the intellect to draw nourishing truth from some scriptural passage or other spiritual source.

So true prayer develops from, but is much more than, discursive reasoning before the Lord, said John. However, progress in true prayer involves ever-deepening purification of the soul through the purgation of both the senses and the spirit. This purification is effected by God through the beginnings of his gift of infused contemplation; thus it is entirely of grace and proceeds from the love of God for his children. We could never even begin to bring about the needed purification ourselves, for our hearts are deceitful and our wills lack the power.

The suffering of the dark night is not ordinary suffering but spiritual pain as the Lord through the Spirit cleanses the soul. It is the necessary condition for movement from the fourth through to the seventh mansions as described by Madre Teresa. John observed that while many souls enter and perhaps pass through the dark night of the senses, they do not even get started on the much more spiritually painful dark night of the spirit. For the first night is like clipping all the tops off the weeds in the garden while the second night is like digging out all their roots. In both cases God himself is the divine gardener and does his work through our attentiveness to him in prayer—even when we do not feel his presence.

For three basic reasons Fray John called this inner, spiritual experience "the dark night." It is an emptying of the soul of its confidence in and search for finite things as ends in themselves; thus it is a "night" for the five senses. Second, the road of prayer is the way of faith, of trusting the promises of God; thus it is a way of darkness for our merely human, worldly ways of thinking. In the third place it is prayer addressed to the God who is beyond all our thoughts, the

God who dwells in inaccessible light, and the God who eternally exists as the transcendent Trinity of Persons. So to us the LORD who is pure, infinite, and eternal Light is perceived as Darkness—not the darkness of evil and sin but, paradoxically, the Darkness of ineffable, endless Light. For in this earthly body that is our best and highest vision. Yet this contemplative union is a transforming union and a union of divine love. The purged soul, illumined by divine truth, is united in love with her Lord and desires to live only for his glory both in the present and for all eternity.

CONCLUSION

We may claim that the Spanish Carmelites, Teresa of Avila and John of the Cross, and the English Puritans, John Owen and Richard Baxter, have much in common. All four, like Augustine and Bernard, are wholly convinced that the chief end of man, the real purpose for which human beings were created and exist, is to enjoy and glorify God for ever. Though they are divided by reason of their allegiance to Roman Catholicism on the one hand and Protestantism on the other, they are united in their love for and delight in the Lord Jesus Christ, King of kings and Lord of lords. All agreed that the highest and deepest form of prayer is that wherein they experience union with God and utter delight in his grace and glory. And all agreed that such knowing and experiencing of God, which leads to holiness of life and to fervor in intercessory and petitionary prayer, does not occur except where one endures purgation or mortification. While much can be found in their writings to set them against each other, it remains true that at a profound level they are in agreement in their contemplating of God in and through Jesus Christ by faith and in love.

CHAPTER 10

The Orthodox Way

A decade or so ago some American evangelicals referred enthusiastically to the Canterbury trail, the route into the Anglican Way—at once evangelical, catholic, and liturgical. If one figure caused this desire for pilgrimage, it was C. S. Lewis, the English scholar, churchman, and apologist.

More recently other evangelicals have referred with similar enthusiasm to the Antioch trail, the route into classic Eastern Orthodoxy through the ancient patriarchate of Antioch (the place where believers in Jesus were first called Christians). The Orthodox Church is seen as supplying all that the Anglican Way seemed to promise but could not deliver because the American Episcopal Church had moved a long way from traditional Anglicanism. For those not particularly attracted to the Antioch trail, perhaps the best-known feature of Orthodox spirituality is that short prayer known as "the Jesus Prayer": "Lord Jesus Christ, Son of God, have mercy upon me, a sinner."

THE JESUS PRAYER

The prayer is obviously based upon the New Testament. "Jesus is Lord" (Phil. 2:11) was the first Christian confession of faith. "Lord," *kyrios*, is the word used in the Greek translation of the Old Testament to convey the name of God, "Yahweh" or "Jehovah." "Jesus" is the name for the Incarnate Son of God that was supplied by the angel from heaven to Joseph (Matt. 1:21). *Christ* is the Greek form of "Messiah," the title of the Deliverer of Israel who fulfilled the Law and the Prophets and redeemed his people. "Son of God" is the title that points to the Holy Trinity and to the Second of the three Persons. "Have mercy upon me" is a petition frequently addressed to God and to Jesus (Luke 18:39), and "mercy" is the word Paul used in Romans 12:1 to refer to all the activity and grace of God toward unworthy sinners.

The Jesus Prayer is now used by many, not only in the Orthodox Church but also in the Roman Catholic and Protestant churches, as a daily form of speaking to the Lord Jesus. Its origins may be traced back to its use by monks of the Orthodox Church (in Egypt and Greece) in the fifth century. The popularity of the prayer in the West is, however, related to the publication of a book, *The Way of a Pilgrim*, the story of an anonymous Russian layman of the nineteenth century who used this prayer profusely and profoundly. I have used this prayer both in a Greek monastery (in the chapel in the company of monks) and privately (as a way of meditation). I commend it to you.

On many occasions during a day we need to pray or ought to pray. When we have a few moments between jobs or while waiting for transport, the Jesus Prayer may be said sincerely and slowly. In a crisis or when facing a problem, we may utter it as a cry to heaven for help. In this manner we are beginning to take seriously the command of the apostle Paul that we "pray without ceasing" (1 Thess. 5:17, KJV).

The recital of the prayer in quiet and concentration

(sitting, standing, or prostrate on the ground) for ten or more minutes is the use that both naturally lends itself to meditation and functions (if God pleases) as the path into the deeper form of prayer that is contemplative and nondiscursive. This "pure" prayer, which dispenses with the imagination and discursive reason, is called *hesychia* by the Greek Orthodox Church.

It is important to realize that the Jesus Prayer is not a Christian mantra; it is not a rhythmic incantation whose words are not important. In saying it we do not aim to suspend all thought (as mantras are used in meditation in Eastern religions) but rather to encounter a Person, even our Lord Jesus Christ. The prayer is addressed to him and embodies a confession of faith within the context of a personal (covenant) relationship.

The repetition of this prayer may seem unacceptable to some people because they recall Jesus' warning in the Sermon on the Mount about "babbling on like pagans," about thinking that "they will be heard because of their many words" (Matt 6:7). Certainly mere repetition is wrong, but do not the angelic hosts repeat the "Holy, Holy, Holy"? The repetition of the Jesus Prayer is to be seen in the light of this angelic, heavenly prayer rather than the babbling of pagans.

Writers from the Orthodox tradition explain that the Jesus Prayer functions at three levels. It is a *prayer of the lips*, recited aloud but not chanted. Beginners are urged to say the words slowly and faithfully, taking care over each word. In the second place it is a *prayer of the mind*; the words are not recited aloud but are pronounced in the quiet of the intellect. Finally, it is a *prayer of the mind in the heart*, that is, of the whole person focused upon God through Jesus Christ. In this third stage, repetition has slowed down, for the heart is bound in a union of love and contemplation to the Lord Jesus.

We can see now that the Jesus Prayer is mental prayer or meditation in both stages one and two. Further, since the right use of this prayer involves the mind concentrating upon the meaning of the words, the more we know of Christ (as he is presented in the New Testament) the better we shall be able to use the Jesus Prayer. Recalling from memory the portrait of Jesus in the four Gospels and the theology of him in the Epistles we shall be able not only to focus upon him imaginatively with the mind's eye but also fill his name ("Lord Jesus Christ, Son of God") with spiritual content. Also we shall be able to put content into *have mercy* and *on me, a sinner* from Christ's teaching and that of his apostles. In this way, as we recite the Jesus Prayer, our affections of gratitude, love, faith, and desire will be aroused and we shall go on to pray with our minds in our hearts.

Thousands of Christians have found that they never grow out of the use of the Jesus Prayer. And the reason why they do not is obvious. The more we read and absorb the sacred Scriptures, the deeper meaning we are able to put into (and also "see") in this prayer. Of course, if we do not nourish our souls in private reading and corporate worship (through Word and Sacrament), we shall find that the frequent recitation of this prayer is not so spiritually productive as when we do actively feed our minds with God's Truth.

Bishop Theophane the Recluse (1815–1894) of the Russian Orthodox Church accurately summed up Orthodox teaching on prayer when he wrote, "The principal thing is to stand before God with the intellect in the heart, and to go on standing before him unceasingly day and night, until the end of life" (cited by S. Bolshakoff in *Russian Mystics*, Kalamazoo, 1977, p. 189). Standing *before God* suggests a personal relationship—that of child and heavenly Father, of sinner and Savior, and of servant and Master. Standing before him *in the heart* suggests an attitude of sincere openness in the very center of our being, the place where Love creates love; further, the placing of the intellect (mind) in the heart means that no opposition is allowed to exist between head and heart, for both are open to, and submitted to, the Lord God.

Finally, standing *unceasingly* suggests that prayer and relationship with God are not for the odd moment but for every moment.

ORTHODOX SPIRITUALITY

The Jesus Prayer is used by Roman Catholics and Protestants in different ways, according to the structure of their devotional life. In Orthodoxy it fits into and serves the path of *theōsis* (deification) and *theōria* (contemplation). This path is usually presented as having three basic strands or elements—not three chronological steps but three intermingling ingredients—*praktikē, physikē,* and *theologia.*

The first element, *praktikē*, is the practice of the Christian virtues or turning away from sinful thought and behavior toward righteousness. It is the purifying of the heart and the loving of God and the neighbor. Further it is (literally) the active life of practicing what is believed. Four basic qualities comprise it: repentance, watchfulness, discrimination, and the guarding of the heart. To repent is to change one's mind concerning self and God and to begin to allow God, as he is known as the Father, the Son, and the Holy Spirit, to be the center of life. In Saint Paul's terms it is to become less and less the servant of sin and more and more the servant of righteousness (Rom 6:15ff.) because in union with Christ Jesus the believer has died to sin and is alive to the God of righteousness.

Watchfulness is to have a sense of direction and purpose, conscious that one is living in God's world and that he is omnipresent. Thus the watchful believer is able to live truly in the present, alert and ready to do the will of God here and now. As Paul Evdokimov put it, "The hour through which you are presently passing, the man whom you meet here and now, the task on which you are engaged at this very moment—these are always the most important in your whole life" (*The Struggle With God*, New Jersey, 1966, p. 67).

Discrimination or discernment is to the spiritual life what the sense of taste is to the physical life. It is the growing ability to know not only what is good or bad but also what is inferior or superior, superfluous or necessary for the soul. Finally, to guard the heart is to protect the soul from yielding to the temptation and provocations of Satan, as these come in a variety of ways. "Above all else, guard your heart, for it is the wellspring of life" (Prov. 4:23). From the heart arise the passions or emotions, and these are to be purified not through eradication but through redirection by the power of the Gospel. They are educated by the teaching of the Holy Spirit.

An important point to appreciate is that the sinful soul that is not penitent and desirous of being like Jesus is the soul that cannot see aright; its moral and spiritual sight is seriously impaired and even nearly totally eliminated. In order to see God we are to be and need to be pure in heart, as Jesus said.

The second element is *physikē*, which is not simply meditating upon nature but rather meditating upon and contemplating God in and through his creation. This is possible because God did not create the world and then abandon it; rather, God sustains the world everywhere and always by being present everywhere. God is invisible to the human eye, but by faith and through faith-knowledge the devout believer begins to see the whole universe as if it were (to recall Moses' experience as recorded in Exodus 3:5) a cosmic burning bush, filled with the divine glow but not consumed.

Such a seeing of God by faith is sight, which only the heart that is being purified may enjoy. It is returning to the original state of the human race before it was corrupted by sin. As Paul expressed it, "Since the creation of the world God's invisible qualities—his eternal power and divine nature—have been clearly seen, being understood from what has been made" (Rom. 1:20). Without genuine *praktikē* there can be no contemplation, and without contemplation God cannot be seen. What all this means was well captured in poetry by the English poet George Herbert in "The Elixir."

> Teach me, my God and King,
> In all things thee to see,
> And what I do in any thing,
> To do it as for thee.
>
> A man that looks on glasse,
> On it may stay his eye;
> Or if he pleaseth, through it passe,
> And then the heav'n espie.

In the second verse two ways of looking at the world are supplied. First, there is a looking that does not see into and through but that sees only the actuality of that which is. Second, there is a looking through the world (as if the world were clear glass) to see God and thus to see all things in God.

This contemplation also includes looking upon human beings in such a way as to see God in and through them as the One in whom they live and move and have their being (Acts 17:28). Further, it is to serve people in such a way that it can be said by the Lord Christ, "Whatever you did for one of the least of these brothers of mine, you did for me" (Matt. 25:40).

The third element is *theologia*, knowing God through Jesus Christ in unmediated union. This form of contemplative prayer may be seen as the dynamic equivalent of what in Roman Catholic teaching is called infused contemplation. It is waiting upon God in silence and awe, overwhelmed by his majesty, held by his love. True theology is not the result of ratiocinative activity but the gazing in adoration on God (*theos*) united to him by his love.

The way that the contemplative prayer of union is described in the literature of Orthodoxy is dependent upon a distinction between the essence of God and the energies of God. There is and cannot by definition be any union of a creature with the essence of God, that is, with the very

Godhead; and there is no unity and cannot by definition be any union of the creature with the Three Persons of the Holy Trinity of the one Godhead. That is, there is no union according to essence (*ousia*) or person (*hypostasis*), but there is union with God's life, power, grace, mercy, and glory (the divine energies). The union is therefore with God as he is toward us rather than with God as he is in himself—with God as he communicates with believers in love rather than God in his inner, trinitarian life. This particular distinction, rarely made in Western theology, extols the very majestic transcendent super-Being of God while also praising and insisting on his immanence and omnipresence in Creation. It affirms God's otherness while proclaiming his nearness.

Orthodox writers often refer to the experience that is *theologia* as knowing God both as light and as darkness. Both God the Father and God the Son are called "Light" in the New Testament, especially in the Johannine gospel and letters. In contemplation God often reveals himself to the one who seeks his face as pure light, the light that is the very presence of God. While saints testify often to this experience, the biblical basis for it is the uncreated light, the divine energy, that was seen in and through Jesus on the mountain where he was transfigured (Matt. 17:2). His face shone and his clothing was aglow with pure light, the uncreated light of God in the energy of light.

Darkness is not perceived as energy of God but as an image that makes clear that our minds are unable to grasp or comprehend the inner nature of God—God as he is in himself. The biblical basis for such thinking is Exodus 20:21, where Moses is described as "approaching the thick darkness where God was." It is important to note that God is said to dwell in darkness and not to be darkness in the same way that he is light. In the path of contemplation the one who truly prays finds that no words or even thoughts are any way near adequate to address or describe God, for God as God is beyond our highest and greatest thoughts. The union with God in his energies is a union of love, not of thought.

Union with God is a union of love with the Holy Trinity and is possible only because the Second Person made human nature his very own, and in that nature healed our sicknesses and cured our diseases through his perfect life, sacrificial death, and glorious resurrection. It is in faith-union with him that Christians can and do experience the presence of God in his energies of grace, holiness, and love. Thereby the process of deification is promoted in them, and they gradually begin to reflect that likeness of God for which they were created.

However, deification (2 Peter 1:4) as total participation in the divine nature (i.e., God in his energies) and the fullness of contemplation (i.e., the everlasting seeing of God in the face of Jesus Christ) await the life of the future kingdom of heaven. Here deification is incomplete and gained slowly, and contemplation as *theologia* is partial and momentary. Yet they are that for which the human being is made and that in which is his true joy and fulfillment.

If we now relate the Jesus Prayer to this threefold dimension of spirituality, it is perhaps clear that we are to locate the third stage of the Jesus Prayer in the contemplation known as *theologia*. The mind is in the heart and the prayer ceases to be deliberately conscious prayer of the one who prays, for in a vital sense it is the prayer of Christ himself in the heart. Thus God is known and experienced as light, love, power, glory, and holiness, even if only for short periods of time, as unceasing prayer arises to God from the mind in the heart.

The Orthodox have a special word for that experience of God in prayer where the mind is without images and concepts and the soul is still and tranquil. It is *hesychia*, and from it come the words *hesychasm* (the practice of contemplative prayer) and *hesychast* (usually a monk who seeks to pray contemplatively. This tradition of prayer, which includes both stillness before God and the open ear to hear what he has to say, can be encountered today in the monasteries on Mount Athos in Greece, or it can be known through its literature, in particular the *Philokalia*. This is a collection of texts written between the fourth and fifteenth centuries by the spiritual masters of the Orthodox tradition.

Before leaving this topic it is perhaps necessary to say that there are other triadic patterns than the one explained above. For example, Gregory of Nyssa, who writes so beautifully of the life of prayer, has three stages in his *The Life of Moses*. Each one corresponds to a self-revelation of God in the Exodus of the Israelites from Egypt to Canaan. The light of the burning bush (Ex. 3:2), the pillar of cloud and of fire (Ex. 13:21), and the darkness on the summit of Mt. Sinai (Ex. 20:21) point to a time of purification in the light, the entry into the contemplation of the intelligibles, and the entry into love in which alone God is known. Then there is the threefold scheme of Denys the Pseudo-Areopagite, which is that of purification, illumination, and union. This has proved to be influential in the West ever since his works were made available in the latter part of the Middle Ages. Most Roman Catholic teaching uses this scheme.

THE CORPORATE EXPERIENCE

In the Roman Catholic and Protestant traditions a close connection obtains between personal contemplation and communal, corporate worship. However, this connection is very clear and important in the Orthodox Church.

The Divine Liturgy (e.g., that of Basil or Chrysostom) by its very nature calls for the contemplative spirit. At the Eucharist what is seen is not merely and only a cultic action performed in and for the church. It is the action of the church itself, for it is the very expression of the life of the church. This is because herein is manifested the new age, the future kingdom of God. The church is certainly in this world to witness for Christ until he comes in glory to judge the living and the dead. However, the church is not of this world, for it is of the future kingdom and reign of God. In the Eucharist that which is above and also of the future, the kingdom, is expressed and manifested in the words, symbols, actions, and life of the Divine Liturgy.

Believers who belong to the age to come are united to Christ by faith and anointed with the Holy Spirit. At and in the Eucharist, the ministry of Word and Sacrament, they are actualized as the new people of God and the body of Christ. They ascend in Christ to be with Christ in his kingdom to be fed by him at his table at the Messianic Banquet with the food that he supplies—his body, the bread of heaven, and his blood, the cup of salvation. It is not that the bread and wine on the holy table become the body and blood of Christ for the faithful. There is an ascent to be with and in Christ, and this occurs because in the Spirit the people of God, the body of Christ, are lifted up into the heavenly realm. The Eucharist expresses and participates in that which belongs to the End (*eschaton*), which is the new life of the coming kingdom of which Jesus Christ is King.

For each believer present within the fellowship of the body of Christ full participation in the ascent to dine at the Lord's table in the kingdom requires repentance and faith certainly—but also the contemplative spirit. There is, in Paul's words, the requirement to set the mind and heart on things above where Christ is (Col. 3:1–2) and to allow Christ to transform and renew each believer as he or she feeds upon him in eucharistic fellowship and union. In this context we see the meaning of the Latin formula, *lex orandi est lex credendi* (what we believe as Christians is based upon what we pray together in the Eucharist). True theology that is contemplative union with God through Jesus Christ is both offered by God through participation in the Eucharist and inspired by the meaning of the Eucharist for the rest of life.

Happily, growing numbers of Western Christians are discovering this ancient, patristic understanding of Christian worship through attendance at or study of the liturgical tradition of the early church as that is still preserved in the Divine Liturgy of the Orthodox churches. To discover this liturgy is also to learn much about mystical contemplation.

CHAPTER 11

Become What You Are!

*A*lready but not yet!

Christian believers are already in Christ and thus are justified, sanctified, and raised into heaven itself in and with him. They have died with him and have also been raised with him. In the reckoning and contemplation of God himself, they are both in Christ and with Christ for eternity. They are the sons of God, fellow heirs with Christ, the unique Son.

Christian believers are living on earth in the Adamic age of sin and death. They have mortal bodies that are polluted by sin and they live as members of a human race that has turned its face away from its Creator. Thus at every turn they face "the world, the flesh, and the devil." Yet they have the firstfruits of the Spirit of Christ in their hearts, and they call God "Abba" for he is their Father in heaven. They meditate upon the revealed Word of God and they enjoy communion with him in prayer, in worship, and in the life of obedience. They look forward to the redemption of their bodies and to becoming in reality what they are already in and with Christ. In the celebration of the Eucharist, they proclaim the Lord who died and lives for evermore as they feed on him in their hearts by faith and in anticipation of that fuller fellowship in the fullness of the kingdom of God.

In the peace and righteousness of the future kingdom of God, the life of believers will be wholly taken up with contemplation—beholding the glory of God in the face of the Lord Jesus Christ—and serving him from one degree of glory to further degrees of glory. Here in their pilgrimage on earth believers are to begin to do that which they shall do for eternity. In the midst of the common round and daily task, in which God is to be honored and praised, they are to meditate upon and contemplate the Lord Jesus Christ in his exalted glory and then to seek to see all things and interpret all life from his perspective. They are to press on by his grace into the maturity of faith, hope, and love. Perfection is their goal, the perfection of divine love.

When Christian believers think of their Lord in heaven and begin to see their life as with and in him, then they begin to talk alike, be they Calvinist Protestant, Tridentine Catholic, or modern pentecostalist charismatic. The greatest experience in life is to know God, who is the Father, the Son, and the Holy Spirit. This is not only knowledge about but knowledge through daily acquaintance with him. Thus whether this communion between the God of the covenant and his adopted children is called meditation, contemplation, or mysticism it is one and the same, for it proceeds from the illumination of the soul by God and returns to the Father through the Son and by the Holy Spirit.

If prayer is the ascent to God of the mind within the heart, then one might think that contemplation is the highest form of prayer—and some have insisted that it is. In that it is actual communing with God, it is truly as high as a sinful mortal can rise. However, if within or from this communing with God, prayers of petition and intercession arise, then one might also say that petitionary prayer is the highest form of prayer. The point I am making is that perhaps to ask the question as to which is the highest or best form of prayer is an inappropriate question to be asking. Believers are to pray, and that is a comprehensive duty!

As one surveys the history of Christian spirituality, it is possible to see two major streams. One is composed of thousands of devout souls who, with little theory but much prayer and in obedience to the Gospel and guided by the Holy Spirit, seek God's face; and as they seek him he meets them and they experience communion with him. Their stories are written in heaven and not too much is known about them here on earth. But these souls are the salt of the earth and the light of the world in their generations. The other stream is much smaller and is composed of those whom we may call the theorists. They not only seek the face of God, but they also reflect upon that experience and seek to lead others into similar mystical knowledge of God in prayer. In this book we have met some of them—Augustine, Denys the Pseudo-Areopagite, Bernard of Clairvaux, Teresa of Avila, John of the Cross, John Owen, and Richard Baxter.

Of course within each stream are differences, for while there is one Mediator, the Lord Jesus Christ, many routes in and through him take the believer to the Father. Even in biblical terms we can say that there is a Pauline, a Petrine, and a Johannine way, and like the colors of the rainbow they are distinct but certainly complementary. Then over the long history of the church various forms of intellectual and affective mysticism and different methods of contemplation and meditation have developed. The great differences between the personalities of the members of the human race probably require a variety of ways of meditative and contemplative prayer. Mysticism does not come in only one package. If it did, only a few would be Christian mystics.

Yet to say all this is not to accept that the mysticism of Christianity is basically of the same nature as other forms of religious mysticism. In Christian mysticism resides a vital sense of the doctrine of *creatio ex nihilo* (creation out of nothing), and thus there is a real sense of the difference between God and the creature. Union with God is always of the will, never of the whole human nature, for the Being of God is wholly different from the beings of humans. Further, the ascent in mind to God (or the descent into the soul to find God) is always for the Christian a way that is in and through the Lord Jesus Christ; we come to God in and by him alone. To claim this is not to deny that the experience of deity claimed by mystics in other religions is wholly false. The Lord God who remains hidden from us except in and through the Light of the world, Jesus Christ, is able to make himself known in partial and fragmentary ways to those who in ascetic contemplation and in sincerity seek the ultimate purpose, meaning, and cause of all life. Following the teaching of Jesus and his apostles, Christians seek the Father only through the Son and in the Holy Spirit.

Therefore the union with the holy Lord God is a oneness of likeness, a oneness of love, and is effected only because of the full involvement of the Holy Spirit. Looked at from the position of the believer, the covenant partner, it is a knowing union. "In thy light I see light" is the experience of the soul (Ps. 36:9). Eternal life is to know the Father and the Son (John 17:3). This cognitive immersion in pure Beauty (for such is the LORD) enthralls and transfigures the soul. The transforming union is also a loving union, wherein (to recall the Song of Songs) the soul kisses God. So tender is the heavenly, affectionate embrace of God that no human tenderness may be compared to it. This love, particularly known in contemplative prayer, runs over into the whole of life so that this love is known and felt throughout the day.

The result of the transforming union with the Lord is certainly that of being spiritually minded or heavenly minded. However, remarkably, this commitment to the invisible kingdom brings with it a right appreciation of the created order and a proper attitude to this world. John of the Cross speaks of a knowing of the creation through the Creator rather than the Creator through the creation:

> The soul is conscious of how all creatures, earthly and
> heavenly, have their life, duration and strength in
> him. . . . Although it is indeed aware that these things
> are distinct from God, insofar as they have created being,
> nonetheless that which it understands of God, by his
> being all these things with infinite eminence, is such
> that it knows these things better in God's being than in
> themselves. And here lies the remarkable delight of this
> awakening: the soul knows creatures through God and
> not God through creatures (*The Living Flame of Love*,
> stanza 4).

This reminds us of the fourth degree of love in the teaching of
Bernard of Clairvaux—the loving of ourselves and our
neighbor in God and for God alone.

My esteemed teacher, Eric Mascall, compared the
attitude toward the world of the worldling and the contemplative:

> What is our attitude to this world to be? Treat it as if it is
> all that there is and as if all that you need is to be found
> in it, and it will dangle its gifts before your eyes, decoy
> you, tantalize you, and finally mock and desert you,
> leaving you empty-handed and with ashes in your
> mouth. But treat it as the creation of God, as truly good
> because it is God's handiwork and yet not the highest
> good because it is not God himself; live in this world as
> one who knows that the world is God's and yet as one
> who knows that his true home is not here but in
> eternity, and the world itself will yield up to you joys
> and splendours of whose very existence the mere
> worldling is utterly ignorant. Then you will see the
> world's transcience and fragility, its finitude and its
> powerlessness to satisfy, not as signs that life is a bad
> joke with man as the helpless victim, but as pale and
> splintered reflections of the splendour and beauty of the
> eternal God—that Beauty ever old and ever new—in
> whom alone man can find lasting peace and joy (*Grace
> and Glory*, 1961, 82).

The reference to Beauty, which is ever old and ever new, is a
citation from Augustine's *Confessions* (X.xvii). To live in and

with Christ in heaven in spirit is to live a godly life here on earth, free to serve God as he wills.

Already but not yet! The call of God to us to become in practical reality what we are already in Christ is a call we need to hear and obey. It is a call to transformation and renewal (Rom. 12:1–2) and will not be answered except by a life of faith and prayer. Those who are justified by faith are called to a life of contemplation!

FOR FURTHER READING

1. On Paul

I recommend the excellent commentaries on Romans by F. F. Bruce (1963), C. E. B. Cranfield (1979), and J. D. G. Dunn (1988). The prayers of Paul are carefully analyzed by Gordon F. Wiles in *Paul's Intercessory Prayers* (1974).

2. On Meditation

Modern books on meditation are often on Eastern meditation. For Christian meditation see Peter Toon, *Meditating As a Christian* (San Francisco, 1991) and *Longing for Heaven* (New York, 1989). The varied books of A. W. Tozer provide examples of the fruit of biblical meditation as do the expository studies of Martyn Lloyd-Jones. Before the Second Vatican Council an abundance of books by Roman Catholics on mental prayer and methods of meditating upon scriptural texts and doctrinal themes was available, but these have dried up in the last two decades as the old discipline has gone out of fashion in modern Western Roman Catholicism. However, one fine recent book on meditation and contemplation is Thomas Dubay's *Fire Within* (San Francisco, 1989).

3. Academic Criticism of Mysticism

Perhaps the best place to start is with Friedrich Heiler's *Prayer: A Study in the History and Psychology of Religion* (London, 1932) and then read the appropriate parts of Anders Nygren's *Agape and Eros*

(London, 1957). References to the criticisms of other writers are found in such defenses of mysticism as Louis Bouyer, *The Christian Mystery* (Edinburgh, 1990); M. C. D'Arcy, *The Mind and Heart of Love* (London, 1945); John Burnaby, *Amor Dei* (London, 1938); Andrew Louth, *The Origins of the Christian Mystical Tradition* (Oxford, 1981); and Grace Jantzen, "Mysticism and Monism" in *The Philosophy in Christianity* (ed. Godfrey Vesey, Cambridge, Eng., 1989).

4. St. Augustine

The works of Augustine are available in a variety of different translations, but since he wrote so much no complete set of his works is in translation. A good selection as a starter is found in *Augustine of Hippo: Selected Writings* (ed. Mary T. Clark, Ramsey, N.J., 1984) and in both *Augustine: Earlier Writings* (ed. John H. S. Burleigh, London, 1953) and *Augustine: Later Writings* (ed. John H. S. Burnaby, London, 1955). Several good modern translations of his *Confessions* are in print, e.g., those by J. K. Ryan (1960), R. S. Pine-Coffin (1974), and V. J. Rourke (1966). I have used the older ones by E. B. Pusey (1838) and F. J. Sheed (1944), often combining them.
John H. S. Burnaby's *Amor Dei* (1938) remains a fine book on Augustine's thought. Cuthbert Butler's *Western Mysticism* (London, 1926) has important sections on Augustine and Bernard and is still very useful.

5. St. Bernard

Both his exposition of the *Canticle* or Song of Songs and *On the Love of God* are available in modern translation in his *Complete Works* (Cistercian Publications, Kalamazoo, 1970–). I used the older translation, *Sermons on the Canticle* (S. J. Beales, 1896).

6. John Owen and Richard Baxter

Owen's *Works* (the edition of W. H. Goold of 1850–1853) have been reprinted in sixteen volumes by the Banner of Truth Trust (Edinburgh, 1964–1970). *On Spiritual Mindedness* is in vol. 7, and his *Meditations on the Glory of Christ* is in vol. 1. Baxter's *Saints'*

Everlasting Rest is in *The Practical Works of Richard Baxter* (Grand Rapids, 1981).

7. Teresa of Avila and John of the Cross

The Complete Works of St. Teresa has been translated by E. Allison Peers in three volumes (New York, 1946), and more recently the Carmelites have published *The Collected Works* (ICS Publications, Washington, D.C., 1974). Likewise the Carmelites have produced *The Collected Works of St. John of the Cross* (ICS, 1979).

8. The Orthodox Way

A valuable series of books is now in process from St. Vladimir's Seminary Press, Crestwood, New York, on the theology and spirituality of the Orthodox churches. For the section on the Eucharist, I made use of the writings of Alexander Schmemann, in particular his *Liturgy and Tradition* (1990).

For the Jesus Prayer I used a variety of writers but followed in particular the English writer Kallistos Ware in *The Power of the Name* (Oxford, 1974) and *The Orthodox Way* (London, 1979). Ware is one of the translators of *The Philokalia* (3 vols., London, 1979–1981).

The Complete Works of Pseudo-Dionysius (Denys), trans. Colm Luibheid (New York, 1987), are fascinating reading for those with a taste for mystical theology. And a useful introduction to Greek Orthodox theology is Constantine N. Tsirpanlis' *Introduction to Eastern Patristic Thought and Orthodox Theology* (Collegeville, Minn., 1991).

INDEX